LUXURY
PRIVATE ISLANDS

LUXURY PRIVATE ISLANDS

edited by Dr. F. Vladi

teNeues

ARCTIC
OCEAN

ASIA

NORTH
PACIFIC
OCEAN

INDIAN
OCEAN

AUSTRALIA

NORTH
AMERICA

EUROPE

**NORTH
ATLANTIC**
OCEAN

AFRICA

**SOUTH
PACIFIC**
OCEAN

SOUTH
AMERICA

**SOUTH
ATLANTIC**
OCEAN

INTRODUCTION

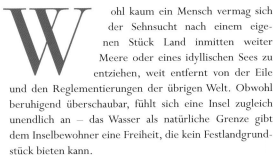

Few people can withstand the longing for their own private piece of land in the midst of vast oceans or an idyllic lake, far from the rush and confinement of the rest of the world. Even though it is of manageable size an island feels infinite—the water creates a natural boundary that provides island dwellers with a freedom not found in any piece of real estate on the mainland.

Yet it is the mainland that gives islands their special character. The luxury of a private island consists of the freedom to escape into solitude and to return from it at any time—therefore, even the smallest island with a simple log cabin is of immense value to its owner.

It is a great and very moving privilege to observe the passing of the season on one's own island. Even after spending many years on their islands, many island owners have described to me how overwhelmed they felt by the beauty and power of nature—and the composure they have learned from it: on an island, everything takes place at nature's own slow pace. Those who respect this pace are richly awarded as they contribute to the maintenance of their island universe.

Islands have cast their spell on me in my childhood, a spell that has not been broken to this day. On March 14, 1971 I sold my first island: Cousine Island in the Seychelles. To this date, the number of islands I have sold has reached 2,000. During these three decades, I had the opportunity to meet island owners with the most varying personalities. Regardless of their profession or social status, they all have one thing in common—they are all extreme individualists with great perseverance when it comes to carrying out their personal endeavors.

Today's island owners do not have to struggle with infrastructure issues anymore. State-of-the-art systems to generate electricity and to purify water, the most comfortable ready-built houses, good technical tools for setting up road systems, as well as electronic communications facilitate the development of the new isle. Once this whole process is completed, the owner usually has built up strong emotional ties to the land.

This remains today's actual major obstacle on the way to purchasing an island—islands are rare, regardless of their location in a lake, a river or the sea.

An island that has been carefully and lovingly reclaimed often feels to its owner like part of the family. Parting company with it is accordingly extremely difficult. This phenomenon can be described in other words: an island does not have a house number. An island has a soul.

Sincerely, Farhad Vladi

Wohl kaum ein Mensch vermag sich der Sehnsucht nach einem eigenen Stück Land inmitten weiter Meere oder eines idyllischen Sees zu entziehen, weit entfernt von der Eile und den Reglementierungen der übrigen Welt. Obwohl beruhigend überschaubar, fühlt sich eine Insel zugleich unendlich an – das Wasser als natürliche Grenze gibt dem Inselbewohner eine Freiheit, die kein Festlandgrundstück bieten kann.

Gerade jedoch das Festland macht die Besonderheit von Inseln erst möglich. Es ist die Freiheit, in die Abgeschiedenheit flüchten und aus ihr zurückkehren zu können, die den Luxus einer Privatinsel ausmacht – schon die kleinste Insel mit einem schlichten Blockhaus ist ihrem Eigentümer daher allergrößter Reichtum.

Es ist ein großes und sehr berührendes Privileg, auf der eigenen Insel die Jahreszeiten kommen und gehen zu sehen. Schon mancher Inselbesitzer berichtete mir noch nach Jahren auf seinem Eiland überwältigt von der Schönheit und Kraft der Natur – und der Gelassenheit, die er von ihr lernte: Auf einer Insel geht alles nur im Schritttempo der Natur; wer sie respektiert, wird in Fülle belohnt, denn er trägt zum Erhalt seiner Inselwelt bei.

Inseln haben mich schon als Kind in ihren Bann gezogen und seither festgehalten. Am 14. März 1971 verkaufte ich mit Cousine Island in den Seychellen meine erste Insel, mittlerweile sind es 2000 geworden. In drei Jahrzehnten habe ich charakterlich unterschiedlichste Inseleigentümer kennen lernen dürfen, die – unabhängig von ihrem Beruf oder gesellschaftlichen Stand – eines gemein haben: Sie alle sind ausgeprägte Individualisten mit einer großen Ausdauer, wenn es um die Erfüllung ihrer persönlichen Vorhaben geht.

Heutige Inseleigentümer müssen sich längst nicht mehr mit Infrastrukturproblemen plagen. Hochmoderne Stromgewinnungs- und Wasseraufbereitungsanlagen, komfortabelste Fertighäuser, gute technische Möglichkeiten zum Anlegen von Verkehrswegen und elektronische Kommunikation erleichtern die Erschließung des neuen Eilands. Ist diese zu einem glücklichen Ende gelangt, hat der Eigentümer meist eine starke emotionale Bindung zu seinem Land entwickelt.

Dies ist heute die eigentlich entscheidende verbliebene Hürde auf dem Wege zum Inselerwerb: Inseln sind rar, ganz gleich ob im See, Fluss oder Meer gelegen. Ein mit viel Liebe erschlossenes Eiland wird für viele Eigentümer zu einer Art Familienmitglied, dieses herzugeben fällt dementsprechend äußerst schwer. Man kann dieses Phänomen auch anders beschreiben: Eine Insel hat keine Hausnummer. Eine Insel hat eine Seele.

Herzlichst, Farhad Vladi

Peu de gens résisteraient à l'envie de se retirer dans un coin de terre leur appartenant au beau milieu des mers ou bien d'un lac idyllique, loin du stress et des réglementations du reste du monde. Même si l'on peut en deviner les contours, une île se perçoit aussi comme un espace sans limites – l'eau qui sert de frontière naturelle donne aux habitants de l'île une liberté que ne peut offrir aucun morceau de continent.

C'est justement le continent qui confère leur particularité aux îles. La liberté de pouvoir fuir dans la solitude et de pouvoir aussi y mettre un terme constitue le luxe d'une île privée – la plus petite des îles flanquée d'une cabane en rondins est la plus grande richesse de son propriétaire.

C'est un privilège important et touchant que de pouvoir regarder défiler les saisons sur son île. Plus d'un propriétaire m'ont déjà raconté qu'ils étaient toujours, des années après, subjugué par la beauté et la force de la nature de leur île – et par le calme qu'ils avaient appris d'elle : sur une île tout évolue au rythme de la nature ; celui qui la respecte est largement récompensé car il participe à la préservation de son univers insulaire.

Enfant déjà, j'étais fasciné par les îles et je suis toujours sous leur emprise. Le 14 mars 1971, j'ai vendu ma première île. Il s'agissait de Cousine Island située dans les Seychelles. Depuis, j'en ai vendu 2 000. En trois décennies, j'ai été amené à rencontrer différents types de propriétaires, lesquels – indépendamment de leur profession et de leur statut social – ont tous un point commun : ce sont de grands individualistes qui font preuve de beaucoup de ténacité quand il s'agit de combler leurs exigences personnelles.

Les propriétaires d'îles actuels n'ont plus à se préoccuper depuis bien longtemps des problèmes d'infrastructure. Les aménagements très modernes pour amener l'eau et l'électricité, les maisons en préfabriqué les plus confortables, les bonnes possibilités techniques d'aménagement des voies d'accès, ainsi que la communication électronique facilitent l'exploitation de la nouvelle île.

Si celle-ci est parvenue à une extrémité heureuse, le propriétaire a généralement développé une forte relation émotionnelle avec son morceau de terre. Ceci est aujourd'hui le seul obstacle décisif qui subsiste concernant la perspective d'acquisition d'une île : qu'elles se situent sur des lacs, des fleuves ou des mers, les îles sont rares. Une île aménagée avec beaucoup d'amour devient pour beaucoup de propriétaires une sorte de membre de la famille dont il est particulièrement difficile de se séparer. On peut aussi décrire ce phénomène autrement : une île n'a pas de numéros de rue. Une île à une âme.

Bien à vous, Farhad Vladi

Prácticamente nadie puede resistirse al anhelo de poseer un pedazo de tierra en medio del ancho mar o de un idílico lago, completamente alejado de las prisas y normas del resto del mundo. Si bien una isla resulta tranquilizadoramente abarcable con la vista, también nos da la sensación de ser infinita –el agua como límite natural otorga al isleño una libertad que ningún terreno de tierra firme puede ofrecerle.

Y sin embargo, la tierra firme es la que hace posible que las islas nos resulten especiales. Es la libertad, el poder evadirse en su retiro y poder volver de él, lo que da cuerpo al lujo de una isla privada –por ello, el más pequeño islote con una sencilla casa de troncos ya representa la mayor de las riquezas para sus propietarios.

Ver pasar las estaciones del año desde su propia isla es un gran privilegio de lo más impresionante. Algunos propietarios, aún años después de su adquisición, me hablan de sus islas, embriagados por la belleza y la fuerza de la naturaleza –y por la tranquilidad aprendida de ella: en una isla todo marcha al paso de la naturaleza; quien la respeta es recompensado con creces, ya que fomenta la conservación de su mundo insular.

Las islas ya me fascinaron desde pequeño y siguen teniéndome atrapado con su encanto. El 14 de marzo de 1971 vendí mi primera isla en las Seychelles con Cousine Island; entretanto, el número de mis ventas asciende a 2000. A lo largo de tres décadas he tenido la oportunidad de conocer a los propietarios de islas de caracteres más diversos, que –independientemente de su profesión o su nivel social– tienen algo en común: todos son individualistas destacados con una gran perseverancia para hacer realidad sus propósitos personales.

Los propietarios de islas de hoy en día ya no tienen que atormentarse con problemas de infraestructura. Las instalaciones de obtención de energía y plantas de tratamiento de agua de lo más modernas, las casas prefabricadas más confortables, buenas posibilidades técnicas para crear vías de tráfico y la comunicación electrónica facilitan la urbanización de la nueva isla. Una vez que ésta haya llegado a buen término, la mayoría de las veces el propietario ya habrá desarrollado un fuerte lazo afectivo con su terreno.

Éste es el verdadero obstáculo determinante que ha subsistido en el camino hacia la compra de una isla: las islas son un bien escaso, independientemente de si se encuentran en lagos, ríos o mares. Una isla urbanizada con mucho cariño se convierte en una especie de miembro de la familia para sus propietarios; consecuentemente, desprenderse de ella es algo realmente duro. Este fenómeno también puede describirse con otras palabras: una isla no tiene número de portal, una isla tiene alma.

Cordialmente, Farhad Vladi

Possedere un angolo di terra circondato dalle acque di mari sconfinati o di un lago idilliaco, lontano dalla fretta e dalle regole imposte dal resto del mondo, è un desiderio comune a molti. Anche se piccola – una cosa tranquillizzante per noi, perché rende più facile l'orientamento – un'isola dà tuttavia un senso di infinito: l'acqua come confine naturale regala una libertà che nessuna terra ferma è in grado di offrire.

Ma è proprio la terra ferma a rendere le isole così particolari. Il lusso di un'isola privata è rappresentato dalla libertà di cercare rifugio nella solitudine e, al contempo, di poterne riemergere. Per questo motivo, anche un'isola molto piccola su cui sorga una semplice capanna in legno rappresenta per il proprietario la più grande delle ricchezze.

Veder scorrere le stagioni sulla propria isola è un privilegio grande ed emozionante. Anche dopo anni di vita sull'isola, più di un proprietario mi ha raccontato di essere ancora sopraffatto dalla bellezza e dalla forza della natura – nonché dalla tranquillità che infonde un luogo in cui tutto si svolge a ritmi naturali: chi rispetta la natura viene ricompensato largamente, perché contribuisce a mantenere intatto il mondo della propria isola.

Sin da bambino le isole hanno esercitato su di me una forte attrazione e ancora oggi esse continuano ad affascinarmi. Il 14 marzo 1971 ho venduto la mia prima isola, Cousine Island, nelle Seychelles; ad oggi, ne ho vendute 2000. Nel corso di trent'anni, ho conosciuto proprietari di isole dal carattere diversissimo che – indipendentemente dalla loro professione o classe sociale – hanno in comune una prerogativa: sono tutti estremamente individualisti, dotati di un'eccezionale tenacia nel perseguire i propri obiettivi.

Ormai i proprietari di isole non devono più affrontare problemi di infrastrutture. Modernissimi impianti di produzione di corrente elettrica e di trattamento delle acque, case prefabbricate assolutamente confortevoli, buone possibilità tecniche per la costruzione di strade e comunicazione elettronica facilitano l'urbanizzazione della nuova isola. Una volta conclusa felicemente questa fase, il proprietario sviluppa generalmente un forte legame emotivo con la sua terra.

L'unico ostacolo determinante all'acquisto di un'isola rimane la rarità di queste terre, non importa se lacustri, fluviali o marine. Un'isola urbanizzata con passione diviene per molti proprietari come un componente della famiglia: rinunciarvi è una cosa estremamente difficile. Si può descrivere questo fenomeno anche in maniera diversa: un'isola non ha un numero civico. Un'isola ha un'anima.

Cordialmente, Farhad Vladi

CONTENTS

Islands:
A Dream of Mankind

Islands have always fascinated humans. During Antiquity, songs were sung about the land surrounded by the sea, the legends of Greek mythology surround the isles around the Peloponnesus. Authors of all eras let their heroes be washed ashore foreign lands. Odysseus and Sinbad are but two of an army of stranded heroes.

Places that seem unattainable and mysterious inspire human imagination. However, since they always required a strenuous trip by ship, islands were considered to be inhospitable for centuries. This is why they were for many years a place to ban prisoners, the sick and other unwanted individuals. Only the occasional shipwrecked person took a refuge in them. Frequently, a returned adventurer spoke proudly of remote islands, which sometimes did not even exist—after all, the discovery of an island guaranteed the status of a hero.

In the 18th century, the image started to change: explorers and artists, philosophers and writers elaborately and romantically praised the landscapes in the sea. Life in Europe's large cities was increasingly dominated by constriction and melancholy, when the heavenly-sounding reports of the French writer Louis-Antoine de Bougainville reached his native continent. The circumnavigator of the globe was interested in a scientific reporting approach and his stories were by no means sailor's yarn. But, following illness and increasing moroseness on board, the stay on Tahiti was to the ship's crew a veritable visit to the Garden of Eden—and de Bougainville transfigured the Polynesian islands to havens of peace and free love, free of jealousy, guilt and sin. Their shores promised singing, welcoming people, sensuously scented gardens and palm trees laden with fruit.

The philosophical basis for a movement of people back to nature was created a few years prior to Bougainville's reports of Tahiti by the French-Swiss state theoretician Jean-Jacques Rousseau. His theory of society's primitive state before the destructive influence of culture fuelled the new desire of the urban society to leave the cheerless cities. Islands seemed to be the perfect refuge in this regard. On them, it was hoped, it would be possible to create the ideal state, similar to the one described by Thomas More in the early 16th century in "Utopia"—a closed harmonious society, leading the perfect life.

The glowing paintings of Paul Gauguin around a century later complemented the image of islands—and Tahiti in particular—as paradise on earth. Gauguin painted gracefully smiling women and lavishly colorful flowers, his paintings spoke of an untamed life. For the yearning individuals, each alluring painting and each effusive word awoke the longing for the perfect place—the myth of the natural island as a place of fulfillment was irrevocably born. To this day, Tahiti remains to be the mother of all places of romantic longings for escape—and all islands of the world are Tahiti's offspring. They are an invitation to dream and linger, a place to escape the hustle and bustle and strains of everyday life.

Those who live in accordance with nature are considered to be patient, learning and wise people. Those who can sustain themselves from their island and the sea surrounding it, feel grateful to the heavens for this gift. Island dwellers master their own fate, setting the rules they live by.

Unannounced visitors are rare. If people do step on the shore, they usually are nature-loving sailors, fishermen or lovers seeking isolation.

Islands are erotic. Nowhere else love is as undisturbed and unmarred as on them; not only in the moonlight are unspoiled beaches the most sought-after setting for romantic scenes and love oaths. Many a dream of children growing up happy and free takes place on islands, that promise shelter far away from all the evil in the world. Already Friedrich Schiller compared the mother's lap to an island with protective shores in "Der spielende Knabe".

Islands thus provide a sense of security: struggles between cultures and religions, turmoil and war, epidemics or famine do not take place in the island dream. At the same time, the isles promise adventure: who visits them is always an explorer and researcher. Daniel Defoe's classic "Robinson Crusoe", which has been translated into almost all languages of the earth, continues to rekindle the love for adventure anew for the past three hundred years.

But islands do not fascinate only adventurers and leisure seekers. They also serve as models for many landscape planners for artificially created land for new living space.

Islands are the site of extremes. On the one hand, people associate them with dark secrets and threatening wilderness, on the other hand they come very close to the human picture of paradise on earth. The thread from which all the legends surrounding islands are spun consists of one part truth, a little hope, a handful of dreams and, last but not least, the old longing for the perfect place.

Martina Matthiesen

Inseln:
ein Menschheitstraum

Inseln faszinieren die Menschen seit jeher. Schon in der Antike wurde das von Meeren umtoste Land besungen, die Sagen der griechischen Mythologie rankten sich um die Eilande rund um den Peleponnes. Autoren aller Epochen ließen die Helden ihrer Geschichten an fremde Ufer spülen. Odysseus und Sindbad stehen für ein Heer von gestrandeten Protagonisten.

Orte, die dem Menschen unerreichbar und geheimnisvoll scheinen, beflügeln seine Phantasie. Allerdings galten Inseln, gerade da es immer einer strapaziösen Bootsreise bedurfte, um sie zu erreichen, jahrhundertelang als unwirtlich. Aus diesem Grund waren sie lange Zeit Orte zur Verbannung von Gefangenen, Kranken und anderen Unerwünschten. Höchstens ein Schiffbrüchiger erkannte in ihnen eine Zufluchtsstätte. Nicht selten sprach ein heimgekehrter Abenteurer stolz von entlegenen Eilanden, die zuweilen gar nicht existierten – schließlich garantierte eine Inselentdeckung den Heldenstatus.

Im 18. Jahrhundert wandelte sich der Blick allmählich: Forscher und Künstler, Philosophen und Literaten ergingen sich in romantischen Lobpreisungen der Landschaften im Meer. Das Leben in den großen Städten Europas wurde zunehmend von Beengtheit und Tristesse geprägt, als die paradiesisch klingenden Berichte des französischen Schriftstellers Louis-Antoine de Bougainville den Heimatkontinent erreichten. Der Weltumsegler war um einen wissenschaftlichen Ansatz bemüht und weit davon entfernt, Seemannsgarn zu spinnen. Doch nach Krankheiten und wachsender Verdrossenheit an Bord bedeutete der Aufenthalt auf Tahiti für die Schiffscrew einen Besuch im Garten Eden – und de Bougainville verklärte die polynesischen Inseln zu Orten des Friedens und der freien Liebe, ohne Eifersucht, Schuld oder Sünde. Ihre Ufer verhießen singende, gastfreundliche Menschen, sinnlich duftende Gärten und fruchtbehängte Palmen.

Den philosophischen Grundstein für eine Bewegung der Menschen zurück zur Natur hatte einige Jahre vor de Bougainvilles Schilderungen Tahitis der französisch-schweizerische Staatstheoretiker Jean-Jacques Rousseau gelegt. Seine Theorie des gesellschaftlichen Urzustandes vor dem zerstörenden Einfluss der Kultur stärkte den neuen Drang der urbanen Gesellschaft hinaus aus den freudlosen Städten. Inseln schienen hierfür der optimale Zufluchtsort zu sein. Auf ihnen, so hoffte man, könne ein idealer Staat möglich sein, wie ihn bereits Thomas Morus Anfang des 16. Jahrhunderts in „Utopia" beschrieb: eine geschlossene, harmonische Gesellschaft, in der ein optimales Leben geführt wird.

Die leuchtenden Gemälde Paul Gauguins etwa ein Jahrhundert später vollendeten schließlich das Bild der Insel – und Tahitis im Besonderen – als Paradies auf Erden. Gauguin malte anmutig lächelnde Frauen und verschwenderisch bunte Blüten, seine Bilder erzählten von einem ungezähmten Leben. In den Sehnsuchtsvollen weckte jedes lockende Gemälde und jedes schwärmende Wort das Bedürfnis nach dem vollkommenen Ort: Der Mythos der ursprünglichen Insel als Stätte der Erfüllung war endgültig geboren. Tahiti ist bis heute die Mutter aller Orte romantischer Sehnsüchte – und alle Inseln der Welt sind Tahitis Kinder. Sie laden zum Träumen und Verweilen ein, hier kann man der Hektik und den Strapazen des Alltags entfliehen.

Wer mit der Natur in Einklang lebt, gilt als geduldiger, lernender und weiser Mensch. Wer sich von seiner Insel und dem Meer herum ernähren kann, fühlt sich dankbar vom Himmel beschenkt. Der Inselbewohner ist sein eigener Herr, er selbst bestimmt die Regeln, nach denen er lebt.

Unangemeldete Besucher gibt es kaum. Und falls doch einmal jemand das Ufer betritt, sind es naturliebende Segler, Fischer oder Einsamkeit suchende Liebende.

Denn Inseln sind erotisch. Nirgends ist die Liebe ungestörter und ursprünglicher, unberührte Strände sind nicht nur im Mondenschein der begehrteste Ort für romantische Beteuerungen und Liebesschwüre. So mancher Traum von glücklich ohne Zwänge aufwachsenden Kindern spielt auf Inseln, die weitab von allem Bösen dieser Welt Geborgenheit versprechen. So setzte schon Friedrich Schiller in „Der spielende Knabe" den Mutterschoß einem Eiland mit schützenden Ufern gleich.

Inseln schenken demnach eine Ahnung von Sicherheit: Kämpfe zwischen Kulturen und Religionen, Aufruhr und Krieg, Epidemien oder Hungersnöte finden im Inseltraum nicht statt. Zugleich verheißen die Eilande auch Abenteuer: Wer sie bereist, ist stets Entdecker und Forscher. Daniel Defoes Klassiker „Robinson Crusoe", der in fast alle Sprachen unserer Welt übersetzt wurde, entfacht die Abenteuerlust seit dreihundert Jahren stets aufs Neue.

Aber nicht nur Abenteurer oder Erholung Suchende sind von Inseln fasziniert. Auch vielen Landschaftsplanern dienen sie als Vorlage für künstlich geschaffenes Land, auf welchem neuer Lebensraum entstehen soll.

Inseln sind extreme Orte, mit denen der Mensch einerseits dunkle Geheimnisse und bedrohliche Wildheit assoziiert, andererseits kommen sie der menschlichen Vorstellung des irdischen Paradieses sehr nahe. Der Faden, aus dem all die Legenden gesponnen sind, die sich um Inseln ranken, besteht aus einem Teil Wahrheit, ein wenig Hoffnung, einer Hand voll Träumen und nicht zuletzt aus der alten Sehnsucht nach dem perfekten Ort.

Martina Matthiesen

Les Îles :
un rêve de l'humanité

Les îles fascinent les hommes depuis toujours. Dès l'Antiquité, ces terres entourées de mer ont été célébrées, et les légendes de la mythologie grecque se sont ancrées autour des îles du Péloponnèse. Les auteurs de toutes les époques laissèrent les héros de leurs histoires accoster sur les rives lointaines. Ulysse et Sindbad représentent une armée de protagonistes échoués.

Les lieux qui paraissent aux hommes inaccessibles et mystérieux stimulent leur imagination. Toutefois, pendant des siècles, les îles ont été considérées comme des lieux inhospitaliers parce qu'on les atteignait au bout d'un épuisant voyage en bateau. Elles ont donc été longtemps le lieu d'exil des prisonniers, des malades et autres indésirables. Seuls les naufragés les considéraient comme un refuge. Il n'était pas rare qu'un aventurier de retour chez lui parle fièrement d'îles isolées qui n'existaient quelquefois même pas. Finalement, la découverte d'une île permettait de gagner le statut de héros.

Au XVIIIᵉ siècle, la perception des îles évolua progressivement : les chercheurs, artistes, philosophes et écrivains se répandirent en louanges romantiques sur les paysages maritimes. Lorsque les récits paradisiaques de Louis-Antoine de Bougainville gagnèrent le continent, la vie dans les grandes villes d'Europe était de plus en plus marquée par l'exiguïté et la tristesse. Parti faire le tour du monde, Bougainville était davantage motivé par une approche scientifique et il n'était guère disposé à raconter des histoires fabuleuses. Pourtant, après avoir souffert de maladies et de lassitude à bord, le séjour à Tahiti sembla être pour l'équipage une visite au jardin d'Éden. Bougainville transfigura les îles polynésiennes en lieux de paix et d'amour libre, sans jalousie, culpabilité ou notion de péché. Leurs rives abritaient des gens accueillants et chantants, des jardins aux odeurs sensuelles et des palmiers pleins de fruits.

Quelques années avant les descriptions de Tahiti de Louis-Antoine de Bougainville, Jean-Jacques Rousseau, théoricien social, avait posé la première pierre philosophique amorçant le retour de l'homme vers la nature. Sa théorie de l'état social initial précédant l'influence destructrive de la culture renforça le nouvel élan de la société urbaine hors des villes sans joie. Les îles parurent alors être le refuge idéal. On espérait qu'elles pouvaient accueillir un État idéal comme l'avait déjà décrit Thomas Morus, au début du XVIᵉ siècle, dans « Utopia » : une société fermée et harmonieuse dans laquelle on menait une vie de rêve.

Les lumineuses toiles de Paul Gauguin, près d'un siècle plus tard, apportèrent la touche finale à la représentation de l'île – Tahiti en particulier – en tant que paradis terrestre. Gauguin peignait des femmes qui souriaient gracieusement et des fleurs hautes en couleurs. Ses peintures relataient une vie indomptable. Chez ceux qui y aspiraient, les peintures séduisantes et les mots pleins d'enthousiasme éveillaient le besoin d'un lieu absolu : le mythe de l'île originelle en tant que lieu de l'accomplissement était enfin né. Tahiti est encore aujourd'hui le lieu des désirs ardents et romantiques, et toutes les îles du monde sont les enfants de Tahiti. Elles invitent à rêver et à y séjourner. Elles permettent de fuir le stress et la fatigue du quotidien.

Celui qui vit à l'unisson avec la nature est considéré comme un être patient, érudit et sage. Celui qui peut se nourrir de son île et de la mer tout autour est reconnaissant du cadeau que lui fait le ciel. L'habitant de l'île est son propre maître, c'est lui qui instaure les règles selon lesquelles il vit.

Il y a peu de visiteurs inattendus. Et si quelques-un abordent les rives, il ne peut s'agir que de certains amoureux de la voile, de pêcheurs ou d'individus aspirant à la solitude.

Car les îles sont érotiques. Nulle part ailleurs l'amour n'est plus authentique et livré à lui-même. Les plages intactes de ces lieux convoités sont adaptées aux promesses romantiques et aux serments d'amour, et pas seulement au clair de lune. C'est ainsi que certains rêves d'enfants heureux et sans contraintes ont lieu sur des îles, lesquelles loin des méchants de ce monde assurent la sécurité. Friedrich Schiller a déjà comparé dans « Der spielende Knabe » le giron maternel à une île aux rives protectrices.

Les îles offrent un sentiment de sécurité : les combats entre les cultures et les religions, la révolte et la guerre, les épidémies et les famines n'ont pas lieu sur un espace insulaire. Mais les îles sont aussi prometteuses d'aventures : celui qui s'y rend est toujours découvreur et chercheur. « Robinson Crusoé », le grand roman de Daniel Defoe qui est traduit dans presque toutes les langues, enflamme continuellement les esprits épris d'aventure depuis plus de 300 ans.

Toutefois, les aventuriers et ceux qui aspirent au repos ne sont pas les seuls à être fascinés par les îles. Ces dernières servent aussi de modèle à de nombreux paysagistes qui créent une terre artificielle sur laquelle doit être conçu un nouvel espace de vie.

Les îles sont des lieux extrêmes auxquels d'une part l'homme associe de sombres mystères et une nature sauvage menaçante, alors que d'autre part, les îles sont très proches de la représentation humaine du paradis sur terre. Le fil conducteur autour duquel sont tissées toutes les légendes qui se déroulent dans les îles est constitué d'une part de vérité, d'un peu d'espoir, d'une poignée de rêves et finalement de cette ancienne nostalgie d'un lieu parfait.

Martina Matthiesen

Islas:
sueño de la humanidad

L as islas han fascinado a los hombres desde tiempos inmemoriales. Ya en la antigüedad, estos pedazos de tierra envueltos por el mar se evocaban en las sagas de la mitología griega, que giraban entorno a las ínsulas que se extendían por el Peloponeso. Autores de todas las épocas han arrastrado a los héroes de sus historias a orillas desconocidas. Odiseo y Simbad son sólo algunos de tantos protagonistas náufragos.

Los lugares que para los humanos parecen inalcanzables y misteriosos son los que dan alas a su imaginación. También es cierto que, durante siglos, el llegar a una isla siempre iba vinculado a la obligación de tener que pasar por un viaje agotador, lo que mermaba su atractivo. De ahí que durante mucho tiempo fueran consideradas como lugares de destierro para presos, enfermos y otros indeseables. Sólo un náufrago podía considerar una isla como refugio. No pocas veces se oían los relatos de aventureros orgullosos al regresar a casa, relatos de ínsulas escondidas, inexistentes en aquellos tiempos. Y es que el mero hecho de descubrir una isla ya convertía en héroe.

En el siglo XVIII esta imagen fue transformándose progresivamente. Investigadores, artistas, filósofos y literatos se sumergían en alabanzas románticas entorno a estos idílicos paisajes en el mar. La vida en las grandes ciudades europeas se impregnaba cada vez más de tristeza y falta de espacio, y al mismo tiempo, llegaban al continente las noticias paradisíacas del escritor Louis-Antoine de Bougainville. Los objetivos de viaje de este navegante universal eran exclusivamente científicos y él no tenía en absoluto la intención de contar batallas imaginarias. Sin embargo, tras la creciente crispación y enfermedades pasadas a bordo, la estancia en Tahití se convirtió para la tripulación en una visita al jardín del Edén. Bougainville aclamó las islas polinesias como el lugar de la paz y el amor libre sin celos, culpa ni pecado. Islas en las que habitaban mujeres y hombres hospitalarios y llenos de júbilo, islas vestidas de jardines sensualmente aromáticos y palmeras cargadas de frutos.

Unos años antes de las descripciones hechas por Bougainville sobre Tahití, el teórico político y social franco-suizo Jean-Jacques Rousseau ya se había encargado de asentar la base filosófica de un movimiento entorno al naturalismo. Su teoría sobre el estado originario, previo a la influencia destructiva de la cultura, incentivó la imperiosa necesidad de la sociedad urbana de escapar de las desalmadas ciudades. Las islas representaban el refugio idóneo. En ellas parecía posible la forma de Estado ideal, como ya lo había descrito Tomás Moro a comienzos del siglo XVI en su obra "Utopía": una sociedad armónica y cerrada en la que se lleva una vida perfecta.

Un siglo más tarde, las luminosas pinturas de Paul Gauguin completaron la imagen de isla, especialmente la de Tahití, como paraíso terrenal. Gauguin pintaba con gracia mujeres sonrientes, flores exuberantes y multicolores. Sus pinturas expresaban una vida sin ataduras. Cada uno de los atractivos cuadros, cada una de las idílicas palabras despertaban en los espíritus ensoñadores , la necesidad de hallar el lugar de perfección absoluta. El mito de la isla primitiva como santuario de la felicidad había nacido definitivamente. Tahití continúa siendo hasta hoy la madre de todos los lugares que persiguen el romanticismo pleno, y todas las islas del planeta son hijas de Tahití.

Todas invitan a soñar y dejar pasar el tiempo. En ellas se disipa la irritación y agotamiento de la vida diaria.

Aquel que vive en comunión con la naturaleza es considerado como persona paciente, con capacidad de aprendizaje y sabiduría. Quien se alimente de su isla y el mar que le rodea, sentirá el gozo de haber recibido un regalo del cielo. El habitante de una isla es su propio señor, y determina él mismo las normas según las que desea vivir.

En una isla apenas se reciben visitas inesperadas. Y en caso de que alguien llegue a la orilla, se tratará de navegantes amantes de la naturaleza, pescadores o parejas en busca de intimidad.

Las islas están cargadas de erotismo. En ningún otro rincón se goza el amor ininterrumpido y original con tanta intensidad. Las playas vírgenes son, no sólo a la luz de la luna, el entorno más deseado para románticas confesiones y declaraciones de amor. Para algunos, el sueño de ver niños felices sin opresiones se hace promesa en las islas, en las que permanecen a salvo de la maldad del mundo. Friedrich Schiller iguala el regazo de la madre a una isla de orillas protectoras en su poema "Der spielende Knabe".

Las islas regalan una idea de protección. En el sueño de isla ideal apenas se producen luchas entre culturas y religiones, apenas hay guerras, epidemias ni hambre. Al mismo tiempo, las islas prometen aventura: quien las alcance es descubridor e investigador de por vida. "Robinsón Crusoe", el clásico de Daniel Defoe, traducido a casi todos los idiomas, revive el apetito de aventura una y otra vez, desde hace trescientos años.

Pero las islas fascinan, no sólo a aventureros y a aquellos en busca del relax. Así mismo numerosos paisajistas las utilizan como base para terrenos artificiales en los que crear un nuevo espacio habitable.

Las islas son lugares extremos, con los que el hombre asocia, por un lado, secretos misteriosos y un estado salvaje amenazante, y por otro la imagen de paraíso terrenal. Los hilos que tejen todas las leyendas entorno a las islas están hechos con un halo de verdad, esperanza, un puñado de sueños y el imperecedero deseo de vivir el lugar perfecto.

Martina Matthiesen

Isole:
un sogno dell'umanità

Da sempre le isole affascinano l'uomo. Fin dall'antichità i poeti hanno cantato di queste terre sulle cui sponde si infrangeva il mare: le isole che circondano il Peloponneso erano lo scenario delle saghe narrate dalla mitologia greca. Autori di tutte le epoche lasciarono approdare su lontani lidi i protagonisti dei loro racconti: Ulisse e Sindbad sono solo due tra tanti eroi naufraghi.

Ciò che appare irraggiungibile e misterioso ha sempre stimolato la fantasia umana. Ma proprio perché si potevano raggiungere solo al termine di faticosi viaggi in mare, le isole hanno avuto per secoli fama di luoghi inospitali e sono state per molto tempo terra di esilio per prigionieri, malati ed altri reietti; solo per i naufraghi esse potevano essere un luogo di salvezza. Al ritorno dalle loro peripezie, non di rado gli avventurieri raccontavano con orgoglio di isole lontane, talvolta inesistenti: la scoperta di un'isola, infatti, garantiva fama di eroe.

Nel corso del XVIII° secolo questo atteggiamento incominciò a cambiare: ricercatori ed artisti, filosofi e letterati iniziarono a tessere romantiche lodi dei paesaggi marini. Allorché i racconti dello scrittore francese Louis-Antoine de Bougainville, ambientati in luoghi paradisiaci, raggiunsero l'Europa, la vita nelle grandi città europee cominciò ad essere percepita come ristretta e triste. L'intento di de Bougainville, che aveva circumnavigato il globo, era di tipo scientifico, ben lontano dal voler raccontare avventure di mare. Ma dopo che a bordo erano scoppiate malattie ed era dilagata una crescente insoddisfazione, la sosta a Tahiti fu per l'equipaggio come una visita nel giardino dell'Eden – e de Bougainville dichiarò che le isole della Polinesia erano un luogo in cui regnavano pace e libero amore, senza gelosia, colpa o peccato. Le loro rive preannunciavano la presenza di gente ospitale che amava il canto, di giardini dai profumi sensuali e di palme cariche di frutti.

Dal punto di vista filosofico, la prima pietra a favore di un ritorno dell'umanità alla natura era stata posta dal pensatore franco-svizzero Jean-Jacques Rousseau, studioso della teoria dello Stato, alcuni anni prima della comparsa dei racconti di de Bougainville su Tahiti. La sua teoria dello stato di natura sociale, minacciato dall'influenza distruttiva della cultura, rafforzò il nuovo impulso della società urbana ad uscire dal grigiore delle città. Le isole sembravano essere un'ottima soluzione; si sperava che su di esse fosse possibile fondare uno Stato ideale, come già Tommaso Moro aveva descritto nella sua "Utopia" all'inizio del XVI° secolo: una società chiusa ed armoniosa, in cui condurre una vita perfetta.

La visione delle isole – Tahiti in particolare – come paradiso in terra fu completata circa un secolo dopo dai luminosi dipinti di Paul Gauguin. Gauguin dipingeva donne dal sorriso ammaliante e miriadi di fiori colorati, raccontando nei suoi quadri le gioie della vita libera. Ogni immagine affascinante ed ogni parola seducente risvegliava negli animi sensibili lo struggente desiderio del luogo perfetto: il mito dell'isola selvaggia come rifugio di felicità era ormai nato. Tahiti è ancora oggi il luogo che simboleggia questo desiderio romantico – e tutte le isole del mondo ne evocano l'atmosfera: esse sono un invito a sognare e a sostare, sono il luogo in cui è possibile sfuggire alla vita frenetica e alle fatiche di ogni giorno.

Coloro che vivono in armonia con la natura sono esseri pazienti, saggi e pronti ad imparare. Chi vive delle risorse della propria isola e del mare che la circonda si sente grato al Cielo per i doni ricevuti. L'abitante dell'isola è padrone di se stesso, è il solo a stabilire le regole che governano la sua vita.

Le visite inattese sono rare. E se qualcuno dovesse approdare, si tratta solo di navigatori amanti della natura, di pescatori o di innamorati in cerca di solitudine.

Le isole, infatti, sono luoghi erotici. In nessun altro posto l'amore è così indisturbato e naturale: quale luogo migliore delle spiagge inviolate – non solo al chiaro di luna – per frasi romantiche e giuramenti d'amore? E che dire dei sogni in cui i bambini giocano felici e crescono senza costrizioni? Spesso tali sogni sono ambientati su un'isola, al sicuro, lontano dal male del mondo. Già Friedrich Schiller ne "Der spielende Knabe" paragonò il grembo materno ad un'isola dalle sponde sicure.

Le isole evocano quindi un senso di sicurezza: conflitti tra culture e religioni, guerre e ribellioni, epidemie o carestie non esistono nel sogno dell'isola felice; allo stesso tempo, le isole promettono avventura: chi vi approda è insieme esploratore e ricercatore. Da trecento anni "Robinson Crusoe", il classico di Daniel Defoe tradotto in quasi tutte le lingue del mondo, ridesta sempre nuova in noi la voglia di avventura.

Ma non soltanto coloro che cercano l'avventura o il riposo sono affascinati dalle isole. Anche molti architetti paesaggisti trovano in esse ispirazione per la creazione di terre artificiali su cui far crescere nuovo spazio vitale.

Le isole sono luoghi estremi, associate, da un lato, ad oscuri segreti ed ai pericoli di una natura selvaggia, dall'altro vicinissime all'idea umana del paradiso terrestre. Il filo di cui sono intessute tutte le leggende che parlano di isole è fatto di una parte di verità, di un po' di speranza, di un pugno di sogni e – non ultimo – dell'antico anelito di un luogo perfetto.

Martina Matthiesen

NORTH AMERICA

FLORIDA

Bonefish Cay

Abaco

Little Whale Cay

Key West

FLORIDA KEYS

Little Hall's Pond Cay

Andros

Musha Cay

THE BAHAMAS

Gulf of Mexico

CUBA

Great Inagua

GREATER ANTILLES

Cayman
Islands

HAITI

DOM.
REP.

MEXICO

JAMAICA

BELIZE

Yucatán Channel

300

PACIFIC
OCEAN

GUATEMALA

HONDURAS

Caribbean Sea

EL
SALVADOR

NICARAGUA

Spanish Water Cay

Curaçao

SOUTH AMERICA

COSTA
RICA

Isla Taborcillo

SOUTH
PACIFIC
OCEAN

Isla
Robinson Crusoe

CHILE

PANAMA

Isla de
Coco

COLOMBIA

210

SOUTH & C

SOUTH AMERICA

60

BRITISH VIRGIN
ISLANDS
Necker Island

Guana Island

90

Barbados

Trinidad

VENEZUELA

THE CARIBBEAN
ENTRAL AMERICA

Bahamas
Musha Cay

Located around 87 miles south-east of Nassau, before Great Exuma Island, Musha Cay is considered to be the world's most luxurious island resort. Oprah Winfrey, Bill Gates, Robin Williams and Steven Spielberg are just a few of the celebrities who escape the limelight for a while on Musha Cay. A staff of thirty is in charge of the well-being of visitors, while internationally-renown top chef prepare culinary masterpieces in the exclusive "The Landings" restaurant—for dinners served directly on the beach to the stimulating backdrop of a spectacular sunset.

Musha Cay, etwa 140 Kilometer südöstlich von Nassau vor der Great Exuma Island gelegen, gilt als das luxuriöseste Insel-Resort der Welt. Oprah Winfrey, Bill Gates, Robin Williams und Steven Spielberg sind nur einige der Prominenten, die sich auf Musha Cay für eine Weile aus dem Rampenlicht zurückziehen. Dreißig Angestellte sind für das Wohl der Gäste zuständig, und internationale Spitzenköche bereiten im exklusiven Restaurant „The Landings" Genüsse der Extraklasse zu – beim Dinner direkt am Meeresstrand, während der Sonnenuntergang für eine stimmungsvolle Kulisse sorgt.

Musha Cay, situé à 140 kilomètres environ au sud-est de Nassau devant la Great Exuma Island est considéré comme le complexe hôtelier insulaire le plus luxueux du monde. Oprah Winfrey, Bill Gates, Robin Williams et Steven Spielberg sont quelques-unes des éminentes personnalités qui viennent séjourner à Musha Cay pour échapper aux feux des projecteurs. Trente employés sont chargés du bien-être des hôtes, tandis que de grands cuisiniers internationaux préparent des plats succulents dans le restaurant distingué, « The Landings ». Il est possible de dîner directement sur la plage avec pour décor le coucher de soleil.

Musha Cay, situada a unos 140 kilómetros al sureste de Nassau, frente a Great Exuma Island, está considerada como el resort isleño más lujoso del mundo. Oprah Winfrey, Bill Gates, Robin Williams y Steven Spielberg son tan sólo algunos de los famosos que optan por evadirse de la prensa durante una temporada en Musha Cay. Treinta empleados se ocupan de garantizar el bienestar de los huéspedes, y chefs de cocina de renombre internacional preparan auténticas delicias en el exclusivo restaurante "The Landings": para gozar de una cena en plena playa, mientras la puesta de sol delinea una espectacular vista.

Musha Cay, situato a circa 140 chilometri a sud di Nassau, di fronte a Great Exuma Island, è considerato il resort più lussuoso mai realizzato su un'isola. Oprah Winfrey, Bill Gates, Robin Williams e Steven Spielberg sono solo alcune delle celebrità che ogni tanto amano ritirarsi a Musha Cay, lontano dalle luci della ribalta. Trenta dipendenti si occupano degli ospiti, mentre cuochi di fama internazionale preparano raffinatissime specialità nell' exclusivo ristorante "The Landings": si cena direttamente sulla spiaggia, nella suggestiva cornice del tramonto.

Seemingly never-ending snowy-white beaches, day beds beneath palm trees, an open lounge, numerous boats, jet skis and diving opportunities, in addition to a tennis court and a fitness center—Musha Cay offers a wide range of individual opportunities for leisurely or active pastimes. Vacationers who enjoy a fairytale-like setting will probably put Musha Cay on the top of their list.

Endlose schneeweiße Strände, Tagesbetten unter Palmen und eine offene Lounge, aber auch zahlreiche Boote, Jetskis und Tauchmöglichkeiten sowie ein Tennisplatz und ein Fitnesscenter – Musha Cay bietet individuelle Möglichkeiten für entspannende oder abwechslungsreiche Stunden. Urlauber mit einem Sinn für das Märchenhafte dürfen Musha Cay ganz oben auf ihre Liste setzen.

Des plages de sable blanc comme neige à perte de vue, des matelas sous les palmiers, un salon ouvert, mais aussi de nombreux bateaux, des jet-skis, des possibilités de faire de la plongée, un court de tennis et un centre de fitness : Musha Cay offre à chacun la possibilité de se détendre et de varier ses activités. Les vacanciers qui ont le goût du merveilleux devraient faire figurer Musha Cay tout en haut de leur liste.

Playas de arena blanca sin fin, tumbonas bajo la sombra de las palmeras y un lounge abierto, además de numerosas embarcaciones, jet skis y oportunidades para practicar el submarinismo, así como una cancha de tenis y un gimnasio: Musha Cay le pone en bandeja las actividades más diversas para disfrutar de unas horas de relax o de diversión. Los turistas apasionados por lugares fantásticos pueden escribir el nombre de Musha Cay en su lista de favoritos.

Spiagge sconfinate e bianchissime, brandine sistemate all'ombra delle palme, una lounge all'aperto, numerose barche, jet-ski e possibilità di immersione, nonché un campo da tennis ed un centro fitness: Musha Cay propone un'infinità di modi di trascorrere ore rilassanti e piacevoli. Musha Cay è il posto ideale per chiunque ami trascorrere vacanze da fiaba.

Bahamas
Little Whale Cay

In the heart of the Bahamas, around 43 miles north of Nassau, there is a 94-acre Garden of Eden: crystal clear water surrounds beaches of soft white sand, flamingos and peacocks roam the subtropical gardens, and butterflies move among hibiscus blossoms—Little Whale Cay is a veritable tropical treasure. The island provides twelve guests with luxury and relaxation coupled with the services of a first-class hotel.

Im Herzen der Bahamas, rund 70 Kilometer nördlich von Nassau, findet sich ein 38 Hektar großer Garten Eden: Kristallklares Wasser umgibt feine, weiße Sandstrände, in den subtropischen Gärten tummeln sich Flamingos und Pfauen, Schmetterlinge flattern um Hibiskusblüten – Little Whale Cay ist ein wahres tropisches Kleinod. Die Insel bietet zwölf Gästen Luxus und Entspannung bei dem Service eines First-Class-Hotels.

Au cœur des Bahamas, à 70 kilomètres au nord de Nassau, se trouve un grand jardin d'Éden d'une superficie de 38 hectares : l'eau limpide entoure de belles plages de sable blanc, dans les jardins subtropicaux s'ébattent des flamands roses et des paons, des papillons volent autour des fleurs d'hibiscus. Little Whale Cay est un véritable joyau tropical. L'île offre à douze hôtes le luxe et la détente dans le cadre du service proposé par un hôtel de première classe.

En el corazón de las Bahamas, a unos 70 kilómetros al norte de Nassau, florece un Jardín del Edén de 38 hectáreas: playas de blanca arena fina rodeadas por agua cristalina, estos jardines subtrópicos son lugar de encuentro para flamencos y pavos reales, las mariposas revolotean alrededor de las flores de hibisco. Little Whale Cay es una auténtica alhaja tropical. La isla mima a doce huéspedes con lujo y relajación gracias al excelente servicio de su hotel de primera clase.

Nel cuore delle Bahamas, a circa 70 chilometri a nord di Nassau, si trova un giardino dell'Eden di 38 ettari: acque cristalline lambiscono spiagge dalla sabbia bianca e fine, fenicotteri rosa e pavoni si aggirano in giardini subtropicali, mentre le farfalle svolazzano attorno ai fiori d'ibisco. Little Whale Cay è un vero gioiello dei tropici. L'isola, dotata del servizio di un hotel di prima categoria, promette lusso e relax a dodici ospiti.

Bahamas
Bonefish Cay

Bonefish Cay is part of the Abacos group of islands. Its name is derived from the abundance of bonefish in the sea surrounding it. Four years of labor and the owner's loving attention to details turned this twelve-acre island into an exclusive hideaway that meets the highest standards. The exclusive furnishings of the three villas and the large main house offer all possible comfort, while a gourmet chef pampers the island guests with creative regional and international delicacies.

Bonefish Cay ist Teil der Abacos-Inselkette und verdankt seinen Namen den reichen Vorkommen an Grätenfischen im umgebenden Meer. Vier Jahre Arbeit und viel Liebe des Eigentümers zum Detail machten dieses fünf Hektar große Eiland zu einem exklusiven Refugium, das höchsten Ansprüchen gerecht wird. Drei Villen und das große Haupthaus bieten mit ihren exklusiven Inneneinrichtungen jeden denkbaren Komfort, und ein Gourmet-Koch verwöhnt die Inselgäste mit phantasievollen regionalen und internationalen Leckereien.

Bonefish Cay fait partie de la chaîne insulaire des Abacos et doit son nom à la forte présence de poissons osseux dans la mer environnante. Quatre années de travail et le grand sens du détail du propriétaire ont fait de cette île de cinq hectares un refuge distingué répondant aux plus grandes exigences. Trois villas et la grande maison principale dont les aménagements intérieurs sont d'un grand raffinement offrent tout le confort souhaité. Un cuisinier gourmet régale les hôtes de l'île en leur servant des délices régionaux et internationaux pleins d'imagination.

Bonefish Cay forma parte del archipiélago de Abacos y debe su nombre a la gran presencia de peces óceos de los mares circundantes. Cuatro años de trabajo y la pasión por los detalles de su propietario han convertido este islote de cinco hectáreas en un refugio de lo más exclusivo, capaz de satisfacer las más altas exigencias. Tres villas y la gran casa principal ofrecen, con sus exclusivos interiores, todo el confort imaginable, y un chef de alta cocina deleita a los huéspedes de la isla con fantásticas exquisiteces regionales e internacionales.

Bonefish Cay fa parte del gruppo delle isole Abacos e deve il nome al bonefish, pesce di cui è ricco il mare circostante. Quattro anni di lavoro e l'attenzione del proprietario per il dettaglio hanno fatto di quest'isola di cinque ettari un rifugio exclusivo, in grado di soddisfare i clienti più esigenti. Tre ville ed una grande casa principale offrono ogni possibile comfort, mentre un cuoco di fama internazionale vizia gli ospiti con prelibatezze tipiche del luogo e specialità estere ricco di fantasia.

Bahamas
Little Hall's Pond Cay

Actor Johnny Depp, his longtime companion Vanessa Paradis, and their two children enjoy the isolation of Little Hall's Pond Cay in the Exuma Cays of the Bahamas. Six white sand beaches and a lagoon ringed with palm trees provide the famous family with a privacy that is hard to come by in their hometown of Los Angeles.

Der Filmschauspieler Johnny Depp, seine Lebensgefährtin Vanessa Paradis und ihre beiden Kinder genießen die Abgeschiedenheit auf Little Hall's Pond Cay in den Exuma Cays der Bahamas. Sechs weiße Sandstrände und eine von Palmen umringte Lagune garantieren der prominenten Familie eine Privatsphäre, die sie in ihrer Heimatstadt Los Angeles kaum finden können.

L'acteur de cinéma, Johnny Depp, sa compagne, Vanessa Paradis et leurs deux enfants profitent de la solitude de Little Hall's Pond Cay dans les Exuma Cays des Bahamas. Six plages de sable blanc et une lagune entourée de palmiers garantissent à cette éminente famille une sphère privée qu'ils ne peuvent trouver dans leur ville de Los Angeles.

El actor de cine Johnny Depp, su compañera Vanessa Paradis y sus dos hijos disfrutan del retiro de Little Hall's Pond Cay, situada en Exuma Cays de las Bahamas. Seis playas blancas y una laguna rodeada de palmeras garantizan a esta familia de famosos una privacidad prácticamente imposible de encontrar en su ciudad, Los Ángeles.

L'attore Johnny Depp, la sua partner Vanessa Paradis ed i loro due figli amano la solitudine di Little Hall's Pond Cay, nelle Exuma Cays delle Bahamas. Sei spiagge dalla sabbia bianca ed una laguna orlata di palme assicurano alla celebre famiglia quella privacy che è impossibile trovare a Los Angeles, dove abitualmente risiede.

British Virgin Islands
Necker Island

The impressive 74-acre Necker Island is surrounded by sandy beaches and coral reefs, it is rarely visited despite the sail boats crossing the horizon. The summit of "Devil's Hill" was cautiously taken down, and its stones were used to build the walls of the Bali-style residential house.

Die imposante Necker Island ist 30 Hektar groß, von feinen Sandstränden und Korallenriffen umgeben und trotz der am Horizont kreuzenden Segelboote selten besucht. Um das Wohnhaus balinesischer Bauart zu errichten, wurde der Gipfel des „Devil's Hill" behutsam abgetragen – und sein Gestein für die Mauern des Hauses verwendet.

L'imposante Necker Island s'étend sur 30 hectares. Elle est entourée de plages de sable fin et de barrières de corail, mais en dépit des voiliers que l'on aperçoit à l'horizon, elle est rarement visitée. Pour la construction de la demeure dans le style balinais, il a fallu aplanir précautionneusement le sommet du „Devil's Hill" – tandis que la roche a été employée pour les murs de la maison.

La superficie de la impresionante Necker Island es de 30 hectáreas, está rodeada de playas de arena fina y arrecifes coralinos, a pesar de los barcos de vela que suelen divisarse en su horizonte, apenas es visitada. Para construir la casa de estilo balinés se aplanó cuidadosamente la cumbre de la "Devil's Hill" y las rocas se emplearon para construcción de los muros.

L'imponente Necker Island, con i suoi 30 ettari di superficie, è orlata di spiagge di sabbia sottile e da scogliere coralline: nonostante l'orizzonte sia solcato da barche a vela di passaggio, i visitatori sono rari. Per la costruzione della casa in stile balinese, la vetta del "Devil's Hill" è stata spianata e la roccia ricavata è stata utilizzata per realizzarne le mura.

Sir Richard Branson is a self-made man par excellence and founder of the British Virgin Group of businesses. But it was not for the name alone that he decided to purchase Necker Island in the Caribbean British Virgin Islands. Each year, Branson spends a several-week vacation with his family and friends on the island—and stays in touch with his internationally networked corporation with the help of cutting-edge telecommunication devices.

Sir Richard Branson ist ein Selfmade-Man par excellence und Gründer des britischen Firmenimperiums Virgin. Doch nicht allein des Namens wegen erwarb er Necker Island in den karibischen Jungferninseln. Mit Familie und Freunden verlebt Branson hier jedes Jahr einen mehrwöchigen Inselurlaub – und bleibt dank modernster Telekommunikation in Kontakt mit seinem international vernetzten Unternehmen.

Sir Richard Branson est le self-made man par excellence et le fondateur de groupe britannique, Virgin. Il a acheté Necker Island aux Caraïbes, dans les îles Vierges britanniques, mais pas seulement en raison du nom. C'est ici, en compagnie de sa famille et de ses amis, que Branson s'accorde plusieurs semaines de vacances insulaires chaque année tout en gardant le contact avec son entreprise internationale grâce à la plus moderne des télécommunications.

Sir Richard Branson es un "selfmade man" por excelencia, y fundador del imperio empresarial británico Virgin. Y sin embargo, no compró la isla de Necker, perteneciente a las caribeñas Islas Vírgenes Británicas, meramente por su nombre. Todos los años, Branson pasa unas vacaciones de varias semanas de duración en esta isla con su familia y amigos, manteniendo el contacto con su empresa internacional gracias a la última tecnología de telecomunicaciones.

Sir Richard Branson, self-made-man per eccellenza, è il fondatore dell'impero di aziende britannico Virgin. Ma non è solo a causa del nome che ha acquistato Necker Island, nelle Isole Vergini Britanniche. Branson trascorre ogni anno più settimane su quest'isola con la famiglia e gli amici, restando in contatto con la propria azienda, connessa a sua volta a livello internazionale, grazie a modernissimi sistemi di telecomunicazione.

Whenever the owner is not staying on Necker Island himself, the luxury resort is rented out to selected guests. Phil Collins, Belinda Carlisle and other famous artists use this paradise as a hideaway; while prominent director Steven Spielberg also enjoys spending carefree days on Necker Island.

Weilt der Besitzer nicht auf Necker Island, wird das Luxus-Resort an erlesene Gäste vermietet: Phil Collins, Belinda Carlisle und andere prominente Künstler nutzen dieses Paradies als Refugium, auch Star-Regisseur Steven Spielberg verbringt hier gern unbeschwerte Tage.

Lorsque le propriétaire ne séjourne pas à Necker Island, le complexe hôtelier de luxe est loué à des hôtes de choix : Phil Collins, Belinda Carlisle et d'autres personnalités du monde des arts considèrent ce paradis comme un refuge. Le metteur en scène renommé Steven Spielberg y passe aussi volontiers des journées insouciantes.

Cuando su propietario no se aloja en la isla de Necker, este resort de lujo se alquila a selectos huéspedes: Phil Collins, Belinda Carlisle y otros artistas de gran renombre se refugian en este paraíso, también el famoso director de cine Steven Spielberg disfruta pasando unos días rebosantes de tranquilidad en este lugar.

Quando il proprietario non soggiorna a Necker Island, questo lussuoso resort viene affittato ad ospiti selezionanati: Phil Collins, Belinda Carlisle e altri noti artisti fanno di questo paradiso il loro rifugio; anche il celebre regista Steven Spielberg trascorre qui sereni periodi di vacanza.

Various important guests from show business and economy became friends and contrived mutual projects on this banquet table.

An dieser festlichen Tafel haben schon allerlei bedeutsame Gäste aus Showgeschäft und Wirtschaft Freundschaften geschlossen und gemeinsame Projekte entwickelt.

Autour de cette table festive, les hôtes importants provenant du show-business et du domaine de l'économie ont déjà noué des amitiés et mis au point des projets communs.

En esta festiva mesa han estechado lazos de amistad famosos huéspedes del mundo del espectáculo y de la economía y han realizado después proyectos conjuntos.

Attorno a questa tavola splendidamente imbandita si sono già incontrati numerosi esponenti dello spettacolo e dell'economia. Sono così nate non solo nuove amicizie, ma anche idee per progetti comuni.

The facilities on Necker Island offer luxurious ambience—integrated in the island's nature. It was carefully constructed from local wood, and is embellished with many native plants. The beach is the guest's casual meeting place for the evening barbecue under the protective ceiling of the treetops.

Die Anlage auf Necker Island bietet ein luxuriöses Ambiente – integriert in die Inselnatur. Sie wurde schonend aus einheimischen Hölzern errichtet und mit vielen einheimischen Pflanzen ausgestattet. Und für das abendliche Barbecue trifft man sich ungezwungen am Strand, als schützendes Dach dienen die Baumkronen.

L'aménagement de Necker Island offre une ambiance somptueuse, intégrée au paysage insulaire. Il a été conçu avec égards pour la nature avec du bois des environs et ornementé de nombreuses plantes de l'endroit. Pour le barbecue, on se retrouve avec décontraction, le soir sur la plage, tandis que le houppier des arbres sert de toit.

Esta instalación en la Necker Island ofrece un lujoso ambiente –integrado en la naturaleza de la isla. La casa fue construida con maderas autóctonas y decorada con una profusión de plantas nativas. Para la barbacoa de la tarde los huéspedes se reúnen en la playa en un ambiente desenfadado; las coronas de los árboles sirven como techo protector.

La struttura realizzata a Necker Island è caratterizzata da un ambiente di lusso perfettamente integrato nella natura dell'isola. Realizzata con legni locali nel pieno rispetto dell'ambiente, è ornata di molte piante originarie del luogo. Per il barbecue serale ci si incontra informalmente sulla spiaggia, sotto le chiome degli alberi.

British Virgin Islands

Guana Island

Just a few minutes by boat from Tortola, Guana Island is located in the deep blue Caribbean Sea. The island's marvelous nature can unfold freely among the thick forests of its 865 acres of hills. Several small, fine stone cottages are found in various places. Their terraces are perfectly suited for breakfasting in the light of an impressive sunrise.

Nur wenige Bootsminuten entfernt von Tortola liegt Guana Island im tiefblauen karibischen Meer. Die prächtige Natur darf sich in den dichten Wäldern der 350 Hektar umfassenden Hänge frei entfalten. Hier finden sich kleine, feine Steincottages, auf deren Terrassen es sich vortrefflich beim beeindruckenden Sonnenaufgang frühstücken lässt.

Guana Island est située à quelques minutes en bateau de Tortola, au beau milieu de la mer des Caraïbes d'un bleu profond. La nature somptueuse peut s'épanouir librement dans les forêts épaisses entourées de 350 hectares de versants. Là se trouvent de petits cottages en pierre raffinés sur la terrasse desquels il est possible de prendre un merveilleux petit-déjeuner devant l'impressionnant lever du soleil.

A tan sólo unos pocos minutos en barco de Tortola se llega a Guana Island, en las aguas azules del Mar Caribe. La exuberante naturaleza se despliega sin límites en los tupidos bosques de las faldas de 350 hectáreas de la isla. Aquí se descubren pequeñas y delicadas casas de campo de piedra, en cuyas terrazas se puede disfrutar de magníficos desayunos e impresionantes amaneceres.

Guana Island è situata a pochi minuti di barca da Tortola, nel blu intenso del Mar dei Caraibi. Una natura spettacolare si presenta in tutte le sue varietà nella fitta foresta che, su una superficie di 350 ettari, abbraccia i pendii. Qui si trovano piccoli, deliziosi cottage di pietra, le cui terrazze invitano a fare colazione nella suggestiva cornice dell'alba.

After spending leisurely hours on one of the extensive beaches of Guana Island or following their favorite exercise—the island offers almost all types of aquatic sports, tennis, golf and crocket—vacationers can withdraw to their cottages among the island's hills and conclude their evening at a dinner with a view of the splendorous ocean.

Nach erholsamen Stunden an einem der weiten Strände von Guana Island oder auch nach sportlicher Betätigung – die Insel bietet fast alle Wassersportarten, Tennis, Golf und Krocket – ziehen sich die Urlaubsgäste in ihre Cottages in den Inselhügeln zurück und lassen den Abend beim Dinner mit hinreißendem Meerblick ausklingen.

Après avoir passé quelques heures reposantes sur l'une des grandes plages de Guana Island ou après les activités sportives – l'île offre la possibilité de pratiquer presque tous les sports nautiques, de même que le tennis, le golf et le croquet – les vacanciers se retirent dans leurs cottages situés au milieu des collines et profitent de la journée qui s'achève en dînant avec une merveilleuse vue sur la mer.

Tras unas horas de relax en una de las amplias playas de Guana, o también tras practicar algún deporte –en la isla se pueden practicar casi todas las modalidades acuáticas, el tenis, golf y crocket–, los huéspedes se refugian en las casas de campo de las colinas isleñas y culminan el día con una cena con impresionantes vistas al mar.

Dopo il relax su una delle grandi spiagge di Guana Island o dopo lo sport – sull'isola è possibile praticare quasi tutti i tipi di sport acquatico, oltre a tennis, golf e croquet – gli ospiti si ritirano nei loro cottage sulle colline dell'isola e trascorrono la serata cenando in terrazza, incantati dalla vista del mare.

Curaçao
Spanish Water Cay

Located around 30 miles north of Venezuela, Curaçao is the largest island of the Dutch Antilles. Its capital Willemstad is part of the UNESCO world cultural heritage. In 1997, when the former owner purchased Spanish Water Cay located in a lagoon on Curaçao, the former plantation island only featured a simple little wooden house that was used by locals for barbecues or weekend trips. Within two years, he transformed the five-acre island in an indigenous, blossoming, tropical garden and had a luxurious Caribbean-style villa erected. The house is surrounded by soft sand beaches that offer hidden spots among the shade provided by the many palm trees.

Curaçao ist die größte Insel der Niederländischen Antillen und liegt etwa 50 Kilometer nördlich von Venezuela. Die Hauptstadt Willemstad zählt zum UNESCO-Weltkulturerbe. Als der vormalige Eigentümer 1997 Spanish Water Cay in einer Lagune von Curaçao erwarb, gab es auf der ehemaligen Plantageninsel nur ein schlichtes kleines Holzhaus, das von Einheimischen für Barbecues oder Wochenendausflüge genutzt wurde. Innerhalb von zwei Jahren verwandelte er die zwei Hektar kleine Insel in einen ursprünglichen, blühenden Tropengarten und ließ eine luxuriöse Villa im karibischen Stil errichten. Rund um das Haus bieten feine Sandstrände mit Schatten spendenden Palmen viele versteckte Plätze.

Curaçao est la plus grande île des Antilles néerlandaises. Elle est située à 50 kilomètres environ au nord du Vénézuéla. Willemstad, la capitale, fait partie du patrimoine culturel mondial de l'UNESCO. Lorsque l'ancien propriétaire a fait l'acquisition de Spanish Water Cay en 1997 dans une lagune de Curaçao, il n'y avait alors sur cette ancienne plantation qu'une petite maison en bois toute simple que les autochtones utilisaient pour faire des barbecues et des excursions le week-end. En l'espace de deux ans, le propriétaire transforma cette petite île de deux hectares en un authentique jardin tropical florissant et fit construire une villa luxueuse dans le style caribéen. Autour de la maison, les plages de sable fin dont les palmiers apportent de l'ombre recèlent d'endroits cachés.

Curaçao es la mayor isla de las Antillas Holandesas, situada a unos 50 kilómetros al norte de Venezuela. Su capital, Willemstad, está considerada como Patrimonio de la Humanidad por la UNESCO. Cuando en 1997 su anterior propietario adquirió Spanish Water Cay en una laguna de Curaçao, en esta antigua isla de plantaciones tan sólo había una sencilla casita de madera que utilizaban los nativos para celebrar barbacoas o realizar excursiones de fin de semana. En un período de dos años, transformó la pequeña isla de dos hectáreas en un jardín tropical en flor, e hizo construir una lujosa villa de estilo caribeño. Las playas de arena fina que rodean la casa, con sus palmeras que proporcionan una agradable sombra, esconden numerosos lugares recónditos.

Curaçao è l'isola più grande delle Antille olandesi ed è situata a circa 50 chilometri a nord del Venezuela. La capitale Willemstad fa parte dell'eredità culturale mondiale dell'UNESCO. Quando, nel 1997, l'ex proprietario ha acquistato Spanish Water Cay, situata in una laguna di Curaçao, l'isoletta, che allora era una piantagione, ospitava solo una capanna di legno, utilizzata dagli abitanti per fare il barbecue o per trascorrervi il week-end. Nel giro di due anni, egli trasformò i due ettari dell'isola in un giardino tropicale fiorito, dal fascino primitivo, e vi fece costruire una lussuosa villa in stile caraibico, circondata da spiagge dalla sabbia finissima e da calette appartate orlate di palme.

Isla de Coco

62 miles south of the capital of Panama City, the enchanted Isla del Coco is situated in the Gulf of Panama. Adventurers can set up their tent in the midst of the tropical nature and experience life in the wild.

100 Kilometer südlich der Hauptstadt Panama City liegt die verwunschene Isla del Coco im Golf von Panama: Abenteurer dürfen hier inmitten der tropischen Pflanzenwelt ihr Zelt aufschlagen und das Leben in der Natur erproben.

À 100 kilomètres au sud de la capitale, Panama City, s'étend l'île enchantée, Isla del Coco, dans le golfe de Panama : les aventuriers peuvent ici monter leur tente au beau milieu de la flore tropicale et faire l'expérience de la vie en pleine nature.

100 kilómetros al sur de la capital Ciudad de Panamá se encuentra la encantadora Isla del Coco, en el Golfo de Panamá: en ella, los aventureros pueden montar su tienda de campaña en medio de una fantástica flora tropical y probar a vivir en plena naturaleza.

100 chilometri a sud della capitale Panama City, nel Golfo di Panama, è situata la misteriosa Isla del Coco: chi ama l'avventura può montare la tenda tra la vegetazione tropicale e vivere nella natura.

Chile
Isla Robinson Crusoe

The Scottish seafarer Alexander Selkirk is generally considered to be the model for Daniel Defoe's hero of the novel "Robinson Crusoe": in the early 18th century, the Scotsman traveled in the South Sea until, following a dispute with his captain, he asked to be abandoned on the lonely island of Más a Tierra. Since 1966 it bears the name of Isla Robinson Crusoe in honor of the brave traveler.

Der schottische Seemann Alexander Selkirk gilt gemeinhin als Vorbild für Daniel Defoes Romanhelden Robinson Crusoe: Der Schotte bereiste Anfang des 18. Jahrhunderts die Südsee, bis er sich nach einem Streit mit seinem Kapitän auf der einsamen Insel Más a Tierra aussetzen ließ. Seit 1966 trägt sie zu Ehren des Tapferen den Namen Isla Robinson Crusoe.

Le marin écossais, Alexander Selkirk, est considéré communément comme le modèle qui a inspiré Daniel Defoe pour son héros, Robinson Crusoé : l'Écossais parcourait les mers du Sud au début du XVIIIᵉ siècle jusqu'au jour où il se fit débarquer sur l'île isolée, Más a Tierra, après une querelle avec son capitaine. Depuis 1966, cette île porte le nom de Isla Robinson Crusoe en l'honneur de cet homme valeureux.

El marinero escocés Alexander Selkirk se consider comúnmente como modelo para el héroe de la novela de Daniel Defoe "Robinson Crusoe": el escocés viajó, a principios del siglo XVIII, al Pacífico meridional, hasta que, tras haberse peleado con su capitán, fue abandonado en la solitaria isla Más a Tierra. Desde 1966, ésta lleva el nombre de Isla Robinson Crusoe en honor al valiente.

Il personaggio di Robinson Crusoe, l'eroe del romanzo di Daniel Defoe, è ispirato alla figura del marinaio scozzese Alexander Selkirk, che all'inizio del XVIII° secolo navigò per i mari del Sud finché, dopo aver litigato con il suo capitano, si lasciò abbandonare sulla solitaria isola Más a Tierra. In onore del coraggioso eroe, dal 1966 essa è stata denominata Isola di Robinson Crusoe.

With a height of about 1000 yards, El Junque is the highest elevation of the mountainous island. More than 100 globally unique types of plants are found on Isla Robinson Crusoe, including giant ferns and orchids. Those seeking adventure can camp out in the Robinson cave, in which, however, Alexander Selkirk probably never lived. For those who want to explore the tracks of the hero of their younger years and love untouched nature, this island represents a wealth of possibilities.

Der 915 Meter hohe El Junque ist die höchste Erhebung der gebirgigen Insel. Über 100 weltweit einzigartige Pflanzenarten finden sich auf der Isla Robinson Crusoe, darunter Riesenfarne und Orchideen. Abenteuerhungrige können in der Robinson-Höhle zelten, in der Alexander Selkirk allerdings vermutlich nie gelebt hat. Wer auf den Spuren seines Helden aus Jugendtagen wandeln möchte und unberührte Pflanzenwelten liebt, für den ist diese Insel ein Eldorado an Möglichkeiten.

Le sommet, El Junque, atteignant 915 mètres de haut est le plus élevé de cette île montagneuse. Plus de 100 espèces de plantes uniques poussent sur Isla Robinson Crusoe, parmi lesquelles des fougères géantes et des orchidées. Les assoiffés d'aventure peuvent camper dans les grottes de Robinson dans lesquelles Alexander Selkirk n'a vraisemblablement jamais vécu. Celui qui veut revenir sur les traces du héros de sa jeunesse et qui aime la nature intacte considérera cette île comme un eldorado.

El Junque, con sus 915 metros de altura, es la elevación más alta de esta isla montañosa. Más de 100 especies vegetales únicas en el mundo habitan en la Isla Robinson Crusoe, entre ellas helechos gigantes y orquídeas. Los amantes de la aventura pueden acampar en la cueva Robinson, en la que, no obstante, Alexander Selkirk presumiblemente no vivió nunca. Quien desee seguir las huellas de su héroe de la infancia y disfrute con una flora virgen, esta isla es un auténtico Eldorado.

El Junque, con i suoi 915 metri, è il punto più alto di quest'isola montuosa. Più di 100 specie di piante uniche al mondo, tra cui felci giganti e orchidee, si trovano sull' Isla Robinson Crusoe. I più avventurosi potranno montare la tenda nella caverna di Robinson, in cui, tuttavia, Alexander Selkirk probabilmente non ha mai vissuto. L'isola è un vero eldorado per tutti quelli che desiderano ritrovare le tracce dell'eroe della loro adolescenza e per gli amanti della foresta vergine.

Panama
Isla Taborcillo

US film star John Wayne owned the island of Taborcillo for more than 20 years. This island is shaped like a crescent and located outside the shore of Panama. Only once his precocious health prevented him from traveling to the island, he sadly decided to sell it in 1977.

Der US-Filmstar John Wayne besaß über 20 Jahre lang die Insel Taborcillo, die, wie ein Halbmond geformt, vor der Küste Panamas liegt. Erst als seine angegriffene Gesundheit die Anreise nicht mehr zuließ, verkaufte er sie im Jahre 1977 schweren Herzens.

La star du cinéma américain, John Wayne, a été propriétaire pendant plus de 20 ans de Isla Taborcillo qui a la forme d'un croissant de lune et qui est située au large de la côte de Panama. Il la vendit à contre-cœur en 1977 lorsque sa santé altérée ne lui permit plus de faire le voyage.

La estrella de cine norteamericana John Wayne fue dueño de la Isla Taborcillo, que con su forma de media luna se erige ante la costa de Panamá, durante 20 años. La vendió en 1977, muy a su pesar, sólo cuando su delicada salud ya no le permitió viajar hasta la misma.

L'attore americano John Wayne è stato per più di 20 anni il proprietario dell'Isla Taborcillo, adagiata come una mezzaluna di fronte alla costa di Panama. Nel 1977, quando le sue condizioni di salute non gli permisero più di recarvisi, John Wayne fu costretto, a malincuore, a vendere l'isola.

PACIFIC
OCEAN

NORTH AMERICA

*East Brother
Island*

San Francisco Bay

California

MEXICO

Gulf of California

CANADA & USA

Hudson
Bay

Newfoundland

CANADA

Lake
Superior

Cabot Strait

*Sleepy Cove
Island*

*Dark
Island*

Nova Scotia

Lake
Huron

Rocky Island

Emerald Isle

Lake
Ontario

*Meissner
Island*

Lake
Michigan

Lake Erie

New York

UNITED STATES
OF AMERICA

60

90

Florida

A T L A N T I C
O C E A N

120

FLORIDA KEYS

Abaco

240

Gulf
of Mexico

Melody Key

THE BAHAMAS

150

CUBA

210

180

SOUTH AMERICA

California

East Brother Island

In the San Pablo Strait which connects San Francisco Bay with the San Pablo Bay, lies East Brother Island, measuring less than an acre. It is dominated by a lighthouse, erected in the 1870s, with an adjacent Victorian-style residential house. In the late 19th and early 20th centuries, the Californian coast featured almost 50 such "light houses" of which only a few remain intact today. A stone throw away is the even smaller barren rock island of West Brother. It is only inhabited by a flock of seagulls.

In der San-Pablo-Meerenge, die die San Francisco Bay mit der San Pablo Bay verbindet, liegt die gerade einen Drittel Hektar große East Brother Island. Sie wird beherrscht von einem in den 1870er Jahren errichteten Leuchtturm mit angeschlossenem Wohnhaus im viktorianischen Stil. Im späten 19. und frühen 20. Jahrhundert gab es fast 50 solcher „Leuchtstationen" an der kalifornischen Küste; nur wenige davon sind erhalten geblieben. Einen Steinwurf entfernt liegt die noch kleinere, kahle Felseninsel West Brother. Ihre einzigen Bewohner sind ein Schwarm Seemöwen.

Dans le détroit de San Pablo qui relie la baie de San Francisco Bay avec celle de San Pablo s'étend la grande East Brother Island, qui mesure juste un tiers d'hectare. Elle est dominée par un phare construit dans les années 1870 avec une maison attenante en style victorien. À la fin du XIXe siècle et au début du XXe, on comptait presque cinquante « stations lumineuses » de ce type sur la côte californienne. Peu d'entre eux ont été préservés. À quelques pas de là se trouve l'île de falaises, dénudée, plus petite encore du nom de West Brother. Les mouettes sont ses seuls occupants.

En el estrecho de San Pablo, que une San Francisco Bay con San Pablo Bay, se encuentra la Isla East Brother Island, con una superficie de tan sólo un tercio de hectárea. Está dominada por un faro construido en los años setenta del siglo XIX con una casa adosada de estilo victoriano. A finales del siglo XIX y principios del XX existían casi 50 faros de este tipo a lo largo de la costa californiana; hoy tan sólo se conservan unos pocos. A tiro de piedra del faro se divisa el aún más pequeño y desértico islote de rocas West Brother. Sus únicos habitantes son una bandada de gaviotas.

Nella San Pablo Strait, che collega la San Francisco Bay alla San Pablo Bay, è situata East Brother Island, la cui superficie raggiunge appena un terzo di ettaro. È dominata da un faro costruito intorno al 1870, con annessa un' abitazione in stile vittoriano. Alla fine del XIXo e agli inizi del XXo secolo, sulla costa californiana esistevano circa 50 fari di questo tipo; oggi ne sono rimasti solo pochi. A breve distanza è situata la brulla isola rocciosa di West Brother, ancora più piccola, i cui unici abitanti sono uno stormo di gabbiani.

Dark Island

F.G. Bourne

The Thousand Islands region between Toronto and Montreal is considered to be among the most beautiful regions of North America. Dark Island is located in the Alexandria Bay of the Saint Lawrence River on the border of the USA and Canada. In the late 19th century, Commodore Frederick G. Bourne, powerful owner of the Singer factories for sewing machines, commissioned the famous architect Ernest Flagg to build a hunting lodge on it that later came to be known as Singer Castle.

Die Thousand-Islands-Region zwischen Toronto und Montreal gilt als eine der schönsten Nordamerikas. Dark Island liegt in der Alexandria Bay des Sankt-Lorenz-Stroms, auf der Grenze zwischen den USA und Kanada. Commodore Frederick G. Bourne, einflussreicher Inhaber der Singer-Nähmaschinenwerke, ließ Ende des 19. Jahrhunderts von dem berühmten Architekten Ernest Flagg das später so genannte Singer Castle als Jagdsitz errichten.

La région des Thousand Islands qui s'étend entre Toronto et Montréal est considérée comme l'une des plus belles d'Amérique du Nord. Dark Island est située dans la Alexandria Bay du fleuve Saint-Laurent, à la frontière entre les États-Unis et le Canada. Commodore Frederick G. Bourne, influent propriétaire des usines de machines à coudre Singer fit appel à la fin du XIXe siècle au célèbre architecte, Ernest Flagg, pour la construction d'un pavillon de chasse, baptisé ultérieurement château Singer.

La tierra de las Thousand Islands situada entre Toronto y Montreal está considerada como una de las regiones más bellas de Norteamérica. Dark Island se encuentra en el valle Alexandria Bay del río de San Lorenzo, en la frontera entre EE.UU. y Canadá. Commodore Frederick G. Bourne, propietario de grandes influencias de la fábrica de máquinas de coser Singer, mandó construir el castillo que más tarde se conocería como Singer Castle al famoso arquitecto Ernest Flagg a finales del siglo XIX, como residencia de caza.

La regione delle Thousand Islands, tra Toronto e Montreal, è considerata una delle più belle dell'America del Nord. Dark Island è situata presso la Alexandria Bay, lambita dalla corrente di San Lorenzo, sul confine tra USA e Canada. Alla fine del XIXo secolo, il commodoro Frederick G. Bourne, l'influente proprietario dell'azienda produttrice di macchine per cucire Singer, fece costruire dal celebre architetto Ernest Flagg il castello che in seguito fu denominato Singer Castle come sede di caccia.

The Scottish castle which Sir Walter Scott described in his novel "Woodstock" was the model for Singer Castle, and even the clock tower with its carillon was reconstructed in every detail. A mystic atmosphere reigns over the castle: secret passageways connect floors and rooms, the dining room features impressive paintings, while a trap door once served to handle unwanted intruders …

Die schottische Burg, die Sir Walter Scott in seinem Roman „Woodstock" beschreibt, diente als Vorlage für das Singer Castle, selbst der Uhrenturm mit Glockenspiel wurde detailgetreu nachgebaut. Eine mystische Atmosphäre liegt über dem Schloss: Geheimgänge verbinden Etagen und Zimmer, im Speisesaal hängen eindrucksvolle Gemälde, eine Falltür stand einst für unerwünschte Eindringlinge bereit …

Le château fort écossais que décrit Walter Scott dans son roman « Woodstock » servit de modèle au Singer Castle, et la tour de l'horloge avec son carillon a même été fidèlement reproduite. Dans le château règne une atmosphère mystique : des couloirs secrets relient les étages et les chambres, des peintures impressionnantes ornent la salle à manger et une trappe servait autrefois à l'accueil des visiteurs indésirables …

El castillo escocés que Sir Walter Scott describe en su novela "Woodstock" se tomó como modelo para construir el Singer Castle, hasta la torre del reloj con carillón se copió con todo detalle. En el castillo reina un ambiente místico: tiene pasadizos secretos que enlazan pisos y habitaciones, en el comedor hay cuadros impresionantes, y en su tiempo hasta hubo una puerta caediza preparada para hacer frente a los visitantes no deseados …

La fortezza scozzese descritta da Sir Walter Scott nel romanzo "Woodstock" è stata il modello per la costruzione del Singer Castle: perfino l'orologio della torre con il carillon è stato fedelmente ricostruito. Un'atmosfera mistica circonda il castello: passaggi segreti collegano i piani e le stanze, in sala da pranzo sono esposti dipinti affascinanti, e per gli intrusi indesiderati, un tempo, era pronta addirittura una botola …

Nova Scotia

Sleepy Cove
Island

Hilly Sleepy Cove Island is located in a quiet bay of the Shubenacadie Grand Lake in Nova Scotia on the eastern coast of Canada. Visitors can enjoy the peace and quiet of the lake on the ten-acre island, which they share only with the tame squirrels and a few ducks. A comfortable log cabin with a fire place, the island's own canoes and a mainland property with a dock promise peaceful vacation days—even though Halifax, the capital of Nova Scotia, is only 90 miles away.

Die hügelige Sleepy Cove Island liegt in einer verschlafenen Bucht im Shubenacadie Grand Lake in Neuschottland an der Ostküste Kanadas. Wer auf der vier Hektar großen Insel die Ruhe des Sees genießt, muss sie nur mit den zahmen Eichhörnchen und einigen Enten teilen. Ein gemütliches Blockhaus mit Kamin, inseleigene Kanus und ein Festlandsgrundstück mit Bootsanleger versprechen friedliche Ferientage – obwohl die Provinzhauptstadt Halifax nur 30 Kilometer entfernt liegt.

L'île vallonnée, Sleepy Cove Island, est située dans la baie calme de Shubenacadie Grand Lake en Nouvelle-Écosse, sur la côte orientale du Canada. Sur l'île de quatre hectares, les promeneurs qui profitent de la tranquillité du lac n'ont à partager l'espace qu'avec les écureuils apprivoisés et quelques canards. Une cabane en rondins avec une cheminée, des canoës appartenant à l'île et un terrain sur le continent pour attacher les bateaux promettent des vacances paisibles, même si, Halifax, capitale de la province, est située à 30 kilomètres seulement de là.

El islote acolinado Sleepy Cove Island se encuentra en una bahía soñolienta, en el Shubenacadie Grand Lake de Nueva Escocia, costa oriental de Canadá. Quien goza de la tranquilidad que emana el lago en esta isla de cuatro hectáreas sólo tiene que compartirla con dóciles ardillas y unos pocos patos. Una confortable casa de troncos con chimenea, canoas propias de la isla y un terreno de tierra firme con un desembarcadero prometen unos días vacacionales de lo más tranquilos –a pesar de que la capital de provincia Halifax se encuentra a tan sólo 30 kilómetros de distancia.

La collinosa Sleepy Cove Island è situata in una tranquilla insenatura del Shubenacadie Grand Lake, nella Nuova Scozia, sulla costa orientale del Canada. Chi sceglie di godere della calma e del mare su quest'isola di quattro ettari, deve dividerli soltanto con alcuni docili scoiattoli e con qualche anatra. Un'accogliente baita con camino, canoe di proprietà dell'isola ed una porzione di terraferma per il rimessaggio delle barche assicurano vacanze tranquille, sebbene il capoluogo Halifax disti soltanto 30 chilometri.

New York State

Emerald Isle

Brooke Shields, actress and beauty idol, lived for several years on the small Emerald Isle in the midst of Chazy Lake in the famous Adirondack Park. The island is connected to the mainland via a tree-lined levee. The manor house, constructed by famous architect Stanford White out of natural rock, is elaborately paneled with precious wood.

Brooke Shields, Schauspielerin und Schönheitsidol, lebte mehrere Jahre auf der kleinen Emerald Isle inmitten des Chazy Lake im berühmten Adirondack Park. Die Insel ist über einen baumgesäumten Damm mit dem Festland verbunden. Das von dem reputierten Architekten Stanford White aus Naturstein errichtete Herrenhaus ist innen aufwändig mit edlem Holz verkleidet.

Brooke Shields, comédienne et idole de beauté, vécut plusieurs années sur la petite Emerald Isle au beau milieu du Chazy Lake, dans le célèbre Adirondack Park. L'île est reliée au continent par l'intermédiaire d'un barrage bordé d'arbres. La maison de maître construite en pierre naturelle par Stanford White, architecte renommé, est somptueusement habillée à l'intérieur de bois précieux.

Brooke Shields, actriz e icono de belleza, vivió varios años en la pequeña isla Emerald Isle, en aguas del lago Chazy Lake, en el famoso parque Adirondack Park. La isla está unida a tierra firme por un dique ribeteado de árboles. El interior de la casa residencial de piedra natural construida por el arquitecto de gran renombre Stanfort White está revestido laboriosamente con madera noble.

L'attrice e idolo di bellezza Brooke Shields ha vissuto per anni nella piccola Emerald Isle, situata al centro del Chazy Lake, nel celebre Adirondack Park. L'isola è collegata alla terraferma da un terrapieno alberato. Gli interni della casa signorile in pietra naturale, costruita dal noto architetto Stanford White, sono riccamente rivestiti di legno pregiato.

Nova Scotia
Rocky Island

The two islands are located inside the protected bay of Beaver Harbour, two hours away from Halifax. Their name is based on the dramatic steep coastline of the larger island; both Rocky Islands are densely wooded and surrounded by pebble beaches and granite rocks.

Die beiden Inseln liegen in der geschützten Bucht von Beaver Harbour, zwei Stunden von Halifax entfernt. Die dramatische Steilküste der größeren Insel ist für die Namensgebung verantwortlich; beide Rocky Islands sind üppig bewaldet und von Kieselstränden und Granitfelsen umgeben.

Les deux îles sont situées dans la baie protégée de Beaver Harbour à deux heures de Halifax. La falaise dramatique de la plus grande des îles leur a donné son nom. Les deux Rocky Islands sont couvertes de forêts luxuriantes et entourées de plages de galets et de falaises de granit.

Estas dos islas se encuentran en la resguardada bahía de Beaver Harbour, a dos horas de Halifax. La dramática costa brava de la isla de mayor tamaño da pie al nombre del archipiélago; las dos islas de Rocky Islands están pobladas de bosques y rodeadas de playas de guijarros y rocas de granito.

Le due isole si trovano nella baia protetta di Beaver Harbour, a due ore di distanza da Halifax. Il loro nome si deve alla ripidissima costa dell'isola maggiore; entrambe le isole hanno una vegetazione lussureggiante e sono circondate da spiagge di ghiaia e da rocce di granito.

Tony Curtis and wife (left) and Farhad Vladi and daughter Natalie (right) in Beverly Hills.

Nova Scotia
Meissner Island

The Mahone Bay with the picturesque little town of Chester is considered to be the most beautiful bay of Nova Scotia. In 1985, Sir Christopher Ondaatje, an avid art collector, successful businessman and travel writer, purchased Meissner Island located there. Ondaatje established his summer residency on the island and enjoys playing tennis matches in his own court—every once in a while with his brother, popular writer and Booker-award recipient Michael Ondaatje ("The English Patient").

Die Mahone Bay mit der malerischen Kleinstadt Chester gilt als die schönste Bucht Nova Scotias. Sir Christopher Ondaatje, ein begeisterter Kunstsammler, erfolgreicher Geschäftsmann und Reiseschriftsteller, kaufte im Jahr 1985 die dort gelegene Meissner Island. Ondaatje erschloss die Insel als Sommersitz und genießt die Tennismatches auf dem eigenen Court – hin und wieder gemeinsam mit seinem Bruder, dem populären Schriftsteller und Booker-Preisträger Michael Ondaatje („Der englische Patient").

La Mahone Bay avec la petite ville pittoresque de Chester est considérée comme la plus belle baie de la Nouvelle-Écosse. Christopher Ondaatje, collectionneur d'art passionné, homme d'affaires à succès et auteur de livres de voyage acheta en 1985 la Meissner Island située ici. Ondaatje aménagea l'île en résidence d'été et profite des matches de tennis sur son propre court, de temps à autre avec son frère, Michael Ondaatje, écrivain populaire et lauréat (« Le patient anglais »).

Mahone Bay, con la pintoresca localidad de Chester, está considerada como la bahía más bella de Nueva Escocia. Sir Christopher Ondaatje, entusiasmado coleccionista de arte, exitoso hombre de negocios y autor de libros de viajes, adquirió Meissner Island, situada en dicha bahía, en 1985. Ondaatje habilitó la isla como residencia estival y disfruta de los partidos de tenis que tienen lugar en su propia cancha –de vez en cuando junto con su hermano, el popular escritor galardonado con el premio Booker Michael Ondaatje ("El paciente inglés").

Mahone Bay, con la pittoresca cittadina di Chester, è considerata la baia più bella di tutta la Nuova Scozia. Sir Christopher Ondaatje, appassionato collezionista d'arte, affarista di successo e scrittore di viaggi, ha acquistato nel 1985 Meissner Island, un'isola della baia. Ondaatje ne ha fatto la sua residenza estiva e gioca di tanto in tanto a tennis con il fratello, il popolare scrittore e vincitore del premio Booker Michael Ondaatje ("Il paziente inglese"), sul campo di sua proprietà.

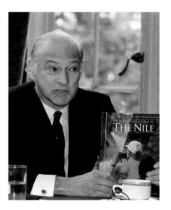

The grand wooden house on Meissner Island was erected in the style of the Nova Scotia province—the delicate-looking yet very robust wooden houses keep the rooms comfortably cool in the summer, and warm in winter. In addition, the durability of these houses is noticeably higher than that of concrete houses. A sailboat almost never fails to appear in photos or paintings of Mahone Bay in Lunenburg County, which is a very popular sailing district. In Nova Scotia, lobster hauling is tradition—locals as well as tourists enjoy this delicacy.

Das herrschaftliche Holzhaus auf Meissner Island wurde im Baustil der Provinz Neuschottland errichtet – die optisch zierlichen und doch äußerst robusten Holzhäuser halten die Räume in den Sommermonaten angenehm kühl und im Winter warm, zudem ist ihre Lebensdauer weit höher als die von Betonhäusern. Auf kaum einem Foto oder Gemälde der Mahone Bay im Lunenburg County fehlt ein Segelboot – sie ist ein beliebtes Segelrevier. Tradition hat in Neuschottland der Hummerfang – frischer Lobster gilt bei den Einheimischen ebenso wie bei den Touristen als Delikatesse.

La somptueuse maison en bois de Meissner Island a été construite dans le style de la province de la Nouvelle-Écosse. La maison à l'aspect raffiné est pourtant exceptionnellement robuste. Cette construction maintient les pièces fraîches en été et conserve la chaleur en hiver. En outre, la durée de vie de ce type de construction est bien supérieure à celle des constructions en béton.
Sur les photographies et peintures représentant la Mahone Bay du Lunenburg County figurent toujours des voiliers. La rivière est effectivement très prisée pour y faire de la voile. La pêche au homard est traditionnelle en Nouvelle-Écosse. Le homard local frais est un mets particulièrement fin tout autant apprécié par les autochtones que par les touristes.

La casa señorial de madera en la Meissner Island fue levantada en la provincia Nueva Escocia. Una casa de madera, ópticamente frágil pero extremadamente robusta, mantiene frescas las estancias en los meses de verano y cálidas en el invierno. Además, su durabilidad es superior a la de las casas de hormigón. En casi ninguna de las fotografías y pinturas de la Mahone Bay en Lunenburg County falta una barca de vela; es una popular zona para practicar este deporte. La pesca de la langosta tiene tradición en Nueva Escocia; el crustáceo de aquí es una delicatesse tanto para los nativos como para los turistas.

La casa padronale di legno di Meissner Island è stata costruita nello stile architettonico tipico della provincia della Nuova Scozia. Una casa di legno, in apparenza leggera ma in realtà estremamente robusta, mantiene le stanze piacevolmente fresche in estate e calde in inverno; la sua durata di vita è inoltre molto più lunga di quella di una costruzione di cemento armato. In quasi tutte le foto o nei dipinti di Mahone Bay, nella Lunenburg County, è visibile una barca a vela: questa è, infatti, una rinomata zona di navigazione. Una tradizione della Nuova Scozia è la pesca dell'astice, prelibata specialità apprezzata sia dagli abitanti del posto sia dai turisti.

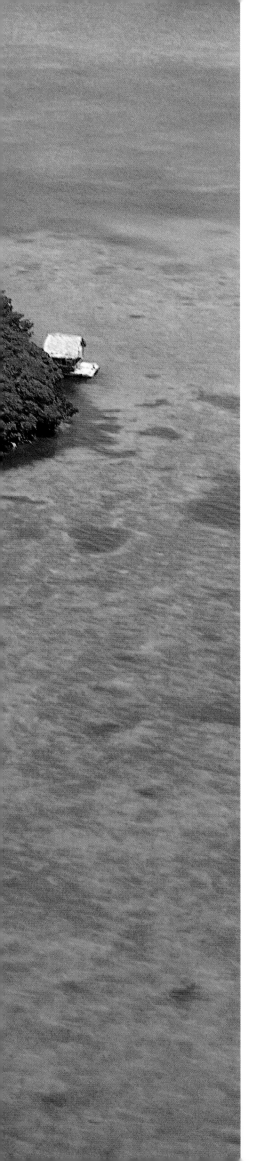

Florida
Melody Key

Nick Hexum, singer of the American rock band 311, purchased the island of Money Key, 25 miles away from Key West in 2004 and had it officially renamed Melody Key in the following year. He wanted to give the island a name that expresses what it is like—a piece of paradise. Whenever Hexum is not using this piece of paradise himself, he rents it out to vacationers.

As opposed to the other inhabited islands of the southern Florida Keys, the indigenous nature has been kept intact on six-acre Melody Key: it contains an abundance of luscious palm trees and scented flowers.

Nick Hexum, Sänger der amerikanischen Rockband 311, kaufte die 40 Kilometer von Key West entfernte Money Key 2004, im Jahr darauf ließ er sie offiziell in Melody Key umbenennen. Er wollte der Insel einen Namen geben, der eher beschreibt, was sie ist: ein Stück vom Paradies. Nutzt Hexum dieses Paradies nicht gerade selbst, lässt er es an Urlaubsgäste vermieten.

Im Gegensatz zu den anderen belebten Inseln der südlichen Florida Keys ist auf der zweieinhalb Hektar großen Melody Key die ursprüngliche Natur erhalten geblieben: Üppige Palmen und duftende Blüten finden sich in Fülle.

Nick Hexum, chanteur du groupe de rock américain 311 a acheté Money Key, située à 40 kilomètres de Key West, en 2004 et l'a rebaptisée officiellement Melody Key. Il voulait donner à l'île un nom qui décrive plutôt ce qu'est un coin de paradis. Quand Hexum ne profite pas lui-même de ce paradis, il le loue à des vacanciers. Contrairement aux autres îles animées des keys sud de la Floride, Melody Key, qui s'étend sur deux hectares et demi, a conservé sa nature d'origine : les palmiers luxuriants et les fleurs parfumées foisonnent ici.

Nick Hexum, cantante del grupo de rock americano 311, le encanta hacer. Compró Money Key, isla situada a 40 kilómetros de Key West, en 2004, y al año siguiente la rebautizó oficialmente como Melody Key. Quería dar a la isla un nombre que describiera mejor lo que es: parte del paraíso. Cuando Hexum no disfruta de este paraíso él mismo, lo alquila a huéspedes vacacionales.

A diferencia de lo que ocurre con otras islas sureñas habitadas de las Florida Keys, en Melody Key, de dos hectáreas y media de extensión, la naturaleza original se mantiene intacta: las exuberantes palmeras y flores perfumadas dominan el paisaje.

Nick Hexum, cantante della rock-band americana 311, ha acquistato Money Key, che dista solo 40 chilometri da Key West, nel 2004; un anno dopo, ha fatto ufficialmente ribattezzare l'isola Melody Key. Voleva dare all'isola un nome che descrivesse quello che è: un angolo di paradiso. Quando non utilizza personalmente questo paradiso, Hexum lo dà in affitto ai villeggianti. Contrariamente alle altre isole Key della Florida meridionale, tutte molto animate, a Melody Key, grande solo due ettari e mezzo, la natura è rimasta intatta, ricca di palme rigogliose e di fiori profumati.

EUROPE

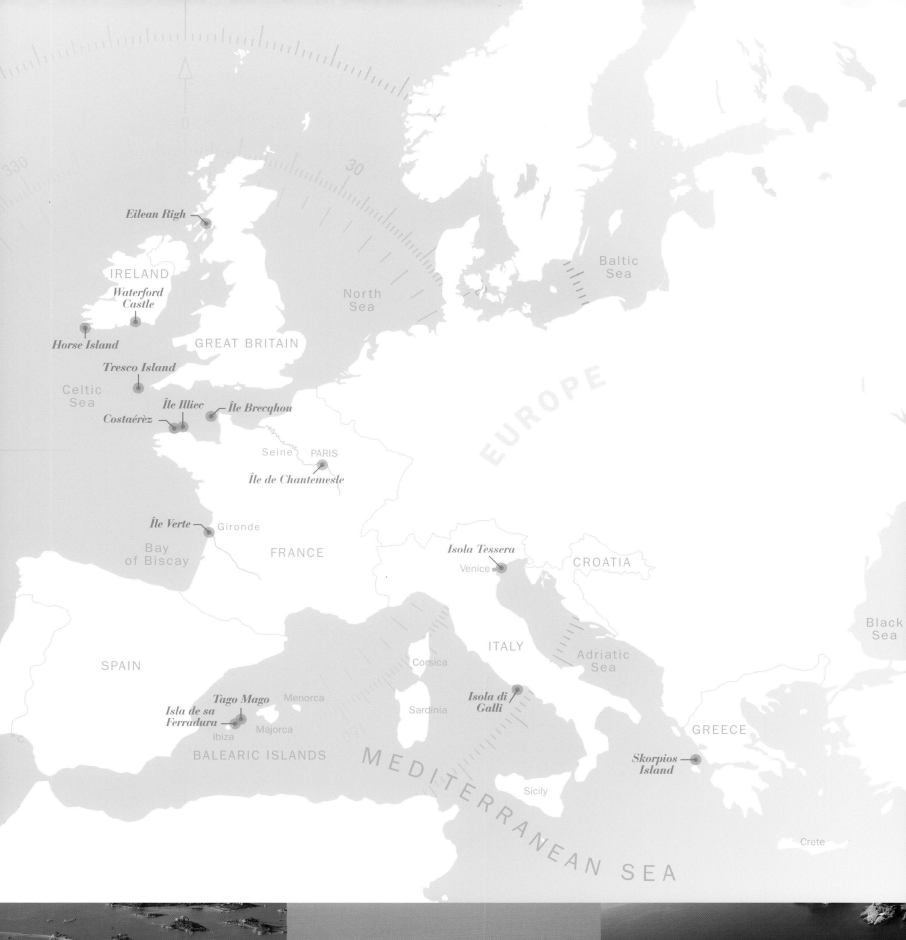

Eilean Righ

IRELAND

Waterford
Castle

North
Sea

Baltic
Sea

Horse Island

GREAT BRITAIN

Tresco Island

Celtic
Sea

Île Illiec — Île Brecqhou

Costaérèz

Seine PARIS

Île de Chantemesle

EUROPE

Île Verte — Gironde

Bay
of Biscay

FRANCE

Isola Tessera

Venice

CROATIA

Black
Sea

SPAIN

Corsica

ITALY

Adriatic
Sea

Tago Mago Menorca

Isla de sa
Ferradura

Sardinia

Isola di
Galli

GREECE

Majorca

Ibiza

BALEARIC ISLANDS

Skorpios
Island

Sicily

MEDITERRANEAN SEA

Crete

AFRICA

Ibiza, Spain
Tago Mago

The spacious private island of Tago Mago lies in a magnificent spot of the Mediterranean. Located only one mile east of the shore of Ibiza, it combines total privacy with the possibility of participating in the lively activities taking place on the neighboring island. The famous Santa Eulalia harbor can be reached in a few minutes by boat. Surrounded by picturesque cliffs, the island has been the property of a European royal family for many years.

In traumhafter Mittelmeerlage findet sich die weitläufige Privatinsel Tago Mago. Sie liegt nur anderthalb Kilometer östlich vor der Küste Ibizas und verbindet absolute Zurückgezogenheit mit der Möglichkeit, am bewegten Leben auf dem Festland teilzunehmen. In wenigen Bootsminuten ist der bekannte Hafen Santa Eulalia erreicht. Die von pittoresken Klippen umsäumte Insel befindet sich seit Jahren in Besitz einer europäischen Fürstenfamilie.

L'île privée et étendue de Tago Mago est située dans un endroit paradisiaque sur la mer Méditerranée, à un kilomètre et demi seulement à l'est de la côte d'Ibiza. Elle associe la solitude absolue à la possibilité de participer à la vie animée du continent. Le célèbre port de Santa Eulalia est situé à quelques minutes de là en bateau. L'île bordée de falaises pittoresques est en possession d'une famille princière européenne depuis de nombreuses années.

En un lugar idílico del Mediterráneo, se encuentra la extensa isla privada de Tago Mago. Situada a tan sólo un kilómetro y medio al oeste de la costa ibicenca, combina un retiro absoluto con la posibilidad de participar en la ajetreada vida balear. En unos pocos minutos de bote, ya se llega al conocido puerto de Santa Eulalia. Desde hace años, esta isla flanqueada de pintorescos arrecifes es propiedad de una familia europea de príncipes.

In magnifica posizione nel Mediterraneo si trova la vasta isola privata di Tago Mago. Situata ad un solo chilometro e mezzo a est di Ibiza, quest'isola unisce alla più assoluta privacy la possibilità di partecipare alla frenetica vita della terraferma. In pochi minuti di barca si raggiunge il noto porto di Santa Eulalia. L'isola, orlata di pittoresche scogliere, è da anni di proprietà di principi europei.

The plans for the recently-erected villa compound on Tago Mago aimed at maintaining the independence of the island's residents as well as providing them with luxurious comfort: electricity generators and sea water desalination plants, a magnificent fresh water pool, and the harmoniously coordinated interior of the residential homes allow the guests to forget the passage of time. A natural harbor with a dock offers protection for the private yachts of the owners.

Die Unabhängigkeit der Inselbewohner stand genauso im Mittelpunkt der Planung des jüngst errichteten Villenkomplexes auf Tago Mago wie der gebotene Komfort: Strom- und Meerwasserentsalzungsanlagen, ein herrlicher Süßwasserpool und das harmonisch aufeinander abgestimmte Interieur der Wohnhäuser lassen die Gäste die Zeit vergessen. Ein natürlicher Hafen mit einem Bootsanleger bietet Schutz für private Yachten der Bewohner.

Le complexe de villas érigé récemment à Tago Mago vise avant tout à préserver tant l'indépendance des habitants de l'île que leur confort : les aménagements de l'électricité et de dessalement de l'eau de mer, la magnifique piscine d'eau douce et l'intérieur harmonisé des demeures permettent aux hôtes de vivre hors du temps. Un port de plaisance naturel abrite les yachts privés des habitants.

Garantizar la independencia de los habitantes de la isla fue tan primordial a la hora de planificar el complejo de villas construido recientemente en Tago Mago como lo fue el confort que debían proporcionar: Las plantas eléctricas y desalinificadoras, una magnífica piscina de agua dulce y el interior totalmente armonioso de las casas de apartamentos hacen que sus huéspedes se olviden del reloj. Un puerto natural con un amarradero para botes protege los yates privados de los isleños.

Scopo della progettazione del complesso di ville recentemente edificato a Tago Mago sono stati sia l'autonomia degli abitanti, sia il comfort: impianti elettrici e di desalinizzazione, una splendida piscina d'acqua dolce e lo stile degli interni, in armonica sintonia gli uni con gli altri, fanno dimenticare lo scorrere del tempo. Un porto naturale con possibilità di rimessaggio per le barche accoglie gli yacht privati degli abitanti.

Isla de sa Ferradura

This island, located just outside the coast of Ibiza, is commonly referred to as "the most beautiful resort in the Mediterranean". It is a fairy-tale setting whose owners have installed every possible luxury and leisure facility possible in an island resort. Subtropical gardens with small waterfalls surround a majestic hacienda; while in a compound of caves guests can enjoy being pampered in a Turkish bath, sauna, solarium and beauty parlor.

„Das schönste Resort im Mittelmeerraum" – dieser Ruf eilt der direkt vor der Küste Ibizas gelegenen Insel voraus. Ein Märchenland, dessen Eigentümer alles verwirklicht haben, was man sich an Luxus und Spielereien für ein Insel-Resort erdenken kann. Subtropische Gärten mit kleinen Wasserfällen umrahmen eine majestätische Hazienda, in einem Höhlenkomplex können sich die Gäste in einem türkischen Bad, in der Sauna, im Solarium und im Kosmetiksalon verwöhnen lassen.

« Le plus splendide complexe hôtelier de la Méditerranée »** – cette réputation vient directement de l'île située au large de la côte d'Ibiza. Un pays merveilleux dont les propriétaires ont réalisé tout ce que l'on peut imaginer en matière de luxe et de passe-temps pour un complexe hôtelier insulaire. Des jardins subtropicaux avec des cascades encadrent une majestueuse hacienda. Dans un complexe de grottes, les hôtes peuvent agréablement profiter du bain turc, du sauna, du solarium et du salon de cosmétique.

"El resort de mayor belleza de todo el Mediterráneo" – esta es la fama de la que goza esta isla situada justo frente a la costa de Ibiza. Un lugar de ensueño cuyos propietarios han puesto en práctica todo lo imaginable en cuanto a lujo y diversión para un resort isleño. Jardines subtropicales con pequeñas cascadas de agua envuelven una majestuosa Hacienda, en un complejo de cuevas los huéspedes pueden deleitarse tomando un baño turco, en la sauna, el solárium o el salón de belleza.

"Il più bel resort del Mediterraneo" è situato proprio di fronte alla costa di Ibiza. Un paese da fiaba, che i proprietari hanno provvisto di ogni lusso e confort immaginabile per il resort di un'isola. Giardini subtropicali e piccole cascate circondano una maestosa hacienda: in un complesso di grotte, gli ospiti possono farsi viziare in un bagno turco, nella sauna, nel solarium e in un salone di bellezza.

Rap star P. Diddy loves Ferradura—because this extraordinary island is a party resort of the highest quality and the singer enjoys plenty of long and unusual partying. All over Ferradura there are bars in which the island's 28 employees invite guests to have a drink, the noble dining room features precious fish in an impressive aquarium, and several fresh water pools are available for a swim. A number of very elegant lounges and a bodega make it difficult to decide where to stay. At the airport guests are already met by a limousine of the island's own car park. When leaving, guest will be hard pushed to state a wish that has not been fulfilled on Isla de sa Ferradura.

Der Rap-Star P. Diddy liebt Ferradura – denn diese außergewöhnliche Insel ist ein Party-Resort der Extraklasse, und der Sänger feiert gerne viel, lang und ausgefallen. Überall auf Ferradura finden sich Bars, an denen einer der 28 Inselangestellten zu einem Drink einlädt, im edlen Dinnerraum tummeln sich kostbare Fische in einem beeindruckenden Aquarium, und mehrere Süßwasserpools laden zum Schwimmen ein. Zahlreiche hochelegante Lounges und eine Bodega erschweren die Entscheidung, wo man verweilen möchte. Schon am Flughafen erwartet den Gast eine Limousine aus dem inseleigenen Fuhrpark. Wer abreist, wird kaum einen Wunsch nennen können, der ihm auf der Isla de sa Ferradura nicht erfüllt wurde.

La star de rap, P. Diddy, aime Ferradura car cette île inhabituelle est un lieu de fête formidable et le chanteur aime beaucoup organiser des fêtes originales et qui durent longtemps. Ferradura compte de nombreux bars situés un peu partout auxquels l'un des 28 employés de l'île invite à boire un verre. Dans la somptueuse salle à manger, des poissons superbes évoluent dans un aquarium impressionnant et plusieurs piscines d'eau douce sont à la disposition des hôtes. Difficile de choisir parmi les nombreux salons extrêmement élégants et la bodega le lieu dans lequel on aimerait passer un moment. Une limousine de l'île attend les hôtes à l'aéroport. Sur Isla de sa Ferradura, les vœux du visiteur sont quasiment tous comblés.

A la estrella del rap P. Diddy le encanta Ferradura: esta isla fuera de lo común es un resort de fiesta de primera clase, y al cantante le gusta celebrar por todo lo alto, hasta la madrugada y de forma bien llamativa. En Ferradura abundan los bares, en los que uno de los 28 empleados de la isla invita a tomar algo, en el refinado comedor los peces de gran valor nadan tranquilamente en un acuario impresionante y diversas piscinas de agua dulce invitan a darse un chapuzón. Un sinnúmero de salones de lo más elegantes y una bodega hacen que tomar la decisión de dónde permanecer no sea nada fácil. En el aeropuerto, una limusina del propio parque de vehículos de la isla ya está esperando para recoger al huésped. Quien abandona la isla prácticamente no puede mencionar ningún deseo que no se haya cumplido en la isla de sa Ferradura.

La star del rap P. Diddy adora Ferradura, perché questa straordinaria isola è un resort per party esclusivi, ed il cantante ama festeggiare spesso, a lungo ed in modo eccentrico. Ovunque a Ferradura si trovano bar in cui uno dei 28 dipendenti dell'isola invita a gustare un drink, pesci rari guizzano nello stupendo acquario dell'elegante sala da pranzo, e molte piscine d'acqua dolce invitano ad una nuotata. Numerose lounge esclusive ed una bodega rendono difficile decidere dove sostare. Già all'aeroporto, una limousine della flotta di veicoli dell'isola attende gli ospiti, mentre chi parte lascia questo luogo con la sensazione che tutti i suoi desideri siano stati esauditi.

Italy
Isola di Galli

In 1989, the legendary ballet dancer Rudolf Nurejew purchased the three Galli islands near the Amalfitan coast from his friend, the choreographer Léonide Massine. Up to his death in the year 1993, the dancer resided primarily on the main island of Isola Lunga in a Venetian-style palace.

The view extends far across the Mediterranean. The region surrounding the picturesque little town of Positano, nestled among towering rocks, is considered to be one of Italy's most beautiful landscapes. Its magic charmed not only Nurejew, but other famous artists as well, including Picasso, Tennessee Williams, John Steinbeck, Elizabeth Taylor and Richard Burton.

Der legendäre Baletttänzer Rudolf Nurejew erwarb 1989 die drei Galli-Inseln an der amalfitanischen Küste von seinem Freund, dem Choreographen Léonide Massine. Bis zu seinem Tod im Jahr 1993 lebte der Tänzer vorwiegend auf der Hauptinsel Lunga in einem venezianisch anmutenden Palast.

Weit schweift der Blick übers Mittelmeer. Die Region um das malerische Städtchen Positano, das sich an hoch aufragende Felsen schmiegt, gilt als eine der schönsten Italiens. Nicht nur Nurejew, sondern auch andere prominente Künstler wie Picasso, Tennessee Williams, John Steinbeck, Elizabeth Taylor und Richard Burton verfielen ihrem Zauber.

Le légendaire danseur de ballet, Rudolf Noureev, acheta en 1989 les trois îles Galli de la côte amalfitaine à son ami et chorégraphe, Léonide Massine. Jusqu'à sa mort en 1993, le danseur vécut sur l'île principale de Lunga dans une demeure semblable à un palais vénitien.

Le regard erre au loin sur la mer Méditerranée. La région qui s'étend autour de la petite ville pittoresque de Positano qui se blottit contre les falaises élevées, est considérée comme l'une des plus belles d'Italie. Outre Noureev, d'autres grands artistes comme Picasso, Tennessee Williams, John Steinbeck, Élisabeth Taylor et Richard Burton tombèrent sous son charme.

En 1989, el legendario bailarín de ballet Rudolf Nurejew compró las tres islas Galli situadas en la costa amalfitana a su amigo, el coreógrafo Léonide Massine. Hasta su muerte, en 1993, el bailarín fijó su residencia habitual en la isla principal Isola Lunga, en un palacio de aire veneciano.

Las vistas hasta el Mediterráneo deleitan la vista. La región entorno a la pequeña ciudad de Positano, aferrada a las altas rocas que sobresalen, está considerada como una de las más bellas de Italia. No sólo Nurejew, sino también otros renombrados artistas como Picasso, Tennessee Williams, John Steinbeck, Elizabeth Taylor y Richard Burton no han sido capaces de resistirse a su encanto.

Il leggendario ballerino Rudolf Nurejew acquistò nel 1989 le tre Isole dei Galli, sulla costiera amalfitana, dal coreografo e suo amico Léonide Massine. Fino alla sua morte, avvenuta nel 1993, il danzatore visse prevalentemente nell'Isola Lunga, la più grande, in un palazzo di stile veneziano.

Lo sguardo spazia sul Mare Mediterraneo. La regione, con la pittoresca cittadina di Positano, arroccata su un'alta scogliera, ha fama di essere una delle più belle d'Italia. Non solo Nurejew, ma anche altri celebri artisti come Picasso, Tennessee Williams, John Steinbeck, Elizabeth Taylor e Richard Burton sono rimasti incantati dal suo splendore.

In 1997, the Galli islands were sold to an Italian hotelier at a price of 3.5 million pounds and the proceeds were donated to Nurejew's charity. Today they are available for rent. In the four-story Saracen tower on Galli, guests reside in nine beautiful rooms and can get a feel of the world of entertainment at the dancer's original ballet studio.

1997 wurden die Galli-Inseln für 3,5 Millionen Pfund an einen italienischen Hotelier verkauft, der Erlös kam der wohltätigen Stiftung Nurejews zugute. Heute werden sie vermietet. Im vierstöckigen Sarazenen-Turm auf der Isola di Galli wohnen Gäste in neun schönen Räumen und können im Original-Ballettstudio Nurejews Bühnenluft atmen.

En 1997, les îles Galli ont été vendues pour 3,5 millions de livres sterling à un hôtelier italien. Le produit de la vente fut reversé à la fondation caritative de Noureev. Aujourd'hui, les îles sont louées. Dans la tour sarrasine de quatre étages, les hôtes vivent dans neuf belles pièces et peuvent respirer l'air de la scène du studio de ballet de Noureev.

En 1997, las islas Galli fueron vendidas por 3,5 millones de libras a un hotelero italiano; esta suma se destinó a la fundación benéfica de Nurejew. En la actualidad, se alquilan. En la torre de los Sarracenos de cuatro plantas de Galli, los huéspedes se alojan en nueve bellas habitaciones y pueden respirar el ambiente de escenario en el estudio de ballet original de Nurejew.

Nel 1997 le Isole dei Galli furono vendute per 3,5 milioni di sterline ad un proprietario di hotel italiano; il ricavato è stato devoluto alla fondazione Rudolf Nurejew. Oggi le isole vengono affittate. Nella torre saracena Isola di Galli, di quattro piani, gli ospiti occupano nove bellissimi vani e possono respirare aria di palcoscenico nello studio di danza di Nurejew.

Italy
Isola Tessera

In a lagoon, close to the heart of Venice, lies the tranquil and calm ravishing little Isola Tessera. It features an 18th century villa and a very beautiful smaller building with two bedrooms, a living room, bathroom and terrace with a view of Venice. Edward de Bono, a British psychologist and writer, has owned Tessera for many years. De Bono is considered to be the leading authority in creative thinking. He published 62 books that were translated into 37 languages—some written on his beloved island that always provides him with the needed peace of mind.

In einer Lagune, dicht vor dem Herzen Venedigs, liegt friedlich und ruhig die hinreißende kleine Isola Tessera. Bebaut ist sie mit einer Villa aus dem 18. Jahrhundert und einem wunderschönen Palais mit zwei Schlafzimmern, Wohnzimmer, Bad und Terrasse – mit Blick auf Venedig. Edward de Bono, britischer Psychologe und Schriftsteller, ist seit vielen Jahren der Eigentümer von Tessera. De Bono gilt als führende Autorität für kreatives Denken. Er veröffentlichte 62 Bücher, die in 37 Sprachen übersetzt wurden – einige entstanden auf seiner geliebten Insel, auf der er immer wieder die nötige Muße findet.

Dans une lagune proche du cœur de Venise, s'étend paisiblement la superbe petite Isola Tessera. Elle abrite une villa datant du XVIIIe siècle et un palais magnifique avec deux chambres à coucher, un salon, une salle de bains et une terrasse avec vue sur Venise. Edward de Bono, psychologue et écrivain britannique, est propriétaire de l'île depuis de nombreuses années. De Bono est considéré comme l'un des maîtres de la pensée créative. Il a publié 62 ouvrages, traduits dans 37 langues. Certains ont même été rédigés sur sa chère île où il vient régulièrement pour se détendre et réfléchir.

En una laguna, muy cerca del corazón de Venecia, reposa, rebosante de paz y tranquilidad, la pequeña y encantadora Isola Tessera. En ella se erigen una villa del siglo XVIII y un maravilloso palacio con dos dormitorios, salón, baño y terraza: con vistas a Venecia. Edward de Bono, psicólogo británico y escritor, es, desde hace muchos años, el propietario de Tessera. De Bono está considerado como la máxima autoridad del pensamiento creativo. Ha publicado 62 libros, traducidos a 37 idiomas: algunos vieron la luz en su querida isla, en la que siempre encuentra de nuevo la inspiración que necesita.

In una laguna, proprio di fronte al cuore di Venezia, è situata, in posizione tranquilla e silenziosa, l'incantevole Isola Tessera. Vi sorge una villa del XVIII° secolo ed un magnifico palazzo con due camere da letto, un salone, un bagno e una terrazza con vista su Venezia. Edward de Bono, psicologo e scrittore britannico, è da molti anni il proprietario di Tessera. De Bono è considerato un'autorità nel campo del pensiero creativo. Ha pubblicato 62 libri tradotti in 37 lingue, alcuni dei quali scritti nella sua amata isola, nella quale, oltre a trascorrere molto tempo libero, ritrova sempre la necessaria ispirazione.

Greece
Skorpios Island

It is said that Aristoteles Onassis collected yachts to be able to visit his beloved islands. The Greek shipowner was most enchanted by Skorpios Island. It was also the location of one of the socially most spectacular weddings of the past century—on October 20, 1968, the billionaire shipowner and Jacqueline Kennedy, widow of the murdered US president John F. Kennedy, were married on Skorpios Island. The wedding took place in the family chapel located in the midst of a cypress grove. During the lifetime of the shipping tycoon, 100 staff members and 20 French chef took care of the family members' needs—Skorpios Island was equipped to cater to every desire of its inhabitants. In 1974, Onassis fell ill with a rare muscle disease of which he died one year later. He was buried in the chapel on the island. In the year 2003, on the occasion of her majority, Onassis' granddaughter Athina inherited the island.

Aristoteles Onassis, so heißt es, sammelte Yachten, um seine geliebten Inseln besuchen zu können. Skorpios hat den griechischen Reeder am meisten bezaubert; sie war auch Ort einer der gesellschaftlich spektakulärsten Hochzeiten des vergangenen Jahrhunderts: Am 20. Oktober 1968 gaben sich der milliardenschwere Reeder und Jacqueline Kennedy, die Witwe des ermordeten US-Präsidenten John F. Kennedy, auf Skorpios das Jawort. Die Trauung fand in der Familienkapelle inmitten eines Zypressenhains statt. 100 Bedienstete und 20 französische Köche sorgten zu Lebzeiten des Tanker-Tycoons für das Wohl des Familienclans – Skorpios war auf jede Laune seiner Bewohner eingerichtet. 1974 erkrankte Onassis an einer seltenen Muskelkrankheit, an der er ein Jahr später starb. Er wurde in der Inselkapelle beigesetzt. Im Jahre 2003, anlässlich ihrer Volljährigkeit, erbte Onassis' Enkelin Athina die Insel.

On raconte qu'Aristote Onassis collectionnait les yachts pour pouvoir visiter ses îles favorites. Mais c'est Skorpios Island qui a le plus charmé l'armateur grec. Elle fut aussi le lieu de l'un des mariages mondains les plus spectaculaires du siècle précédent : le 20 octobre 1968, s'unirent l'armateur milliardaire et Jacqueline Kennedy, la veuve du Président des États-Unis assassiné John F. Kennedy. Le mariage fut célébré dans la chapelle familiale au milieu d'un bois de cyprès. 100 d'employés de maison et 20 cuisiniers français s'activaient du vivant du magnat du transport maritime pour le bien-être du clan familial. Skorpios Island était aménagée pour répondre à toutes les exigences de ses habitants. En 1974, Onassis fut atteint d'une maladie musculaire rare et en mourut un an plus tard. Il fut enterré dans la chapelle de l'île. En 2003, Athina, la petite-fille de Onassis, hérita à sa majorité de l'île.

Aristóteles Onassis, cuentan, coleccionaba yates para poder visitar sus queridas islas. Skorpios Island fue la isla que más fascinó al naviero griego; también fue escenario de una de las bodas de sociedad más espectaculares del siglo pasado: el 20 de octubre de 1968 el naviero multimillonario y Jacqueline Kennedy, viuda del presidente norteamericano asesinado John F. Kennedy, se dieron el "sí, quiero" en la isla de Skorpios Island. La ceremonia se celebró en la capilla familiar, en pleno bosque de cipreses. Un servicio compuesto por 100 personas y 20 cocineros franceses se ocupó del bienestar del clan familiar mientras vivió el magnate naviero: Skorpios Island había sido preparada para poder adaptarse a todos los estados de ánimo de sus habitantes. En 1974 Onassis contrajo una rara enfermedad muscular, de la que falleció un año más tarde. Se le dio sepultura en la capilla de Skorpios Island. En 2003, al cumplir la mayoría de edad, Athina, la nieta de Onassis, heredó la isla.

Si racconta che Aristotele Onassis, collezionasse yacht per poter raggiungere le proprie amate isole. Skorpios Island ha incantato l'armatore greco più di tutte le altre. Essa è stata anche il luogo in cui si è svolto uno degli eventi sociali più spettacolari del secolo scorso: qui il 20 ottobre 1968 l'armatore miliardario sposò Jacqueline Kennedy, la vedova del presidente americano assassinato John F. Kennedy. La cerimonia ebbe luogo nella cappella di famiglia in mezzo ad un boschetto di cipressi. Ai tempi dell'armatore, 100 dipendenti e 20 cuochi francesi erano al servizio del clan, e Skorpios Island era attrezzata per soddisfare ogni desiderio dei suoi abitanti. Nel 1974 Onassis fu colpito da una rara malattia muscolare, e un anno dopo morì. Fu sepolto nella cappella di Skorpios Island. Nel 2003, raggiunta la maggiore età, la nipote Athina ha ereditato l'isola.

France, Seine

Île de Chantemesle

Giverny

The picture-book Île de Chantemesle is located in one of the most charming regions around Paris, between La Roche Guyon and Vétheuil. The Impressionists already felt inspired and touched by the beauty of this landscape. Claude Monet lived and worked here and created important works. The artist continuously discovered new perspectives of Vétheuil, the banks of the Seine and his beloved water lilies in the garden of his house in Giverny. The Île de Chantemesle consists of a ten acres park with magnificent trees. Two spacious villas are located in the midst of magnificently flowering rhododendron hedges; one for the use of island visitors, while the other houses the domestic staff.

Die Bilderbuchinsel Chantemesle befindet sich in einer der bezauberndsten Regionen um Paris, zwischen La Roche Guyon und Vétheuil. Schon die Impressionisten fühlten sich von der Schönheit dieser Landschaft inspiriert und angezogen. Claude Monet lebte und arbeitete hier und schuf bedeutende Werke – Vétheuil, die Seine-Ufer und die geliebten Seerosen im Garten seines Hauses in Giverny entdeckte der Künstler in immer neuem Licht. Die Île de Chantemesle ist ein vier Hektar großer, mit herrlichen Bäumen bewaldeter Park. Zwei großzügige Villen finden sich inmitten zauberhaft blühender Rhododendronhecken, eine steht den Inselgästen zur Verfügung, die andere beherbergt die Hausangestellten.

L'île pittoresque de Chantemesle se situe dans l'une des plus charmantes régions à proximité de Paris, entre La Roche Guyon et Vétheuil. Les impressionnistes ont été inspirés et attirés par la beauté du paysage. Claude Monet a vécu et travaillé sur l'île et y a peint des œuvres importantes. L'artiste a découvert Vétheuil, les bords de Seine et les chers nénuphars du jardin de sa maison de Giverny sous une lumière sans cesse différente. L'île de Chantemesle est un grand parc d'une superficie de quatre hectares où l'on trouve des arbres splendides. Deux villas spacieuses se dressent au milieu de belles haies de rhododendrons. L'une des villas est mise à la disposition des hôtes, tandis que l'autre héberge les employés de maison.

La isla de ensueño Chantemesle se encuentra en una de las regiones más encantadoras de los alrededores de París, entre La Roche Guyon y Vétheuil. Los pintores impresionistas ya se inspiraron y sintieron atraídos por la belleza de este paisaje. Claude Monet vivió y trabajó aquí, y pintó obras importantes –el artista descubrió, con una luz siempre diferente, Vétheuil, la orilla del Sena y los apreciados nenúfares del jardín de su casa de Giverny. Île Chantemesle es un parque de cuatro hectáreas poblado por magníficos árboles. Dos espléndidas villas se erigen en medio de hermosos arbustos de rododendros en flor; una de ellas está disponible para los huéspedes de la isla, mientras que la otra alberga a los empleados domésticos.

La fiabesca Île de Chantemesle si trova in una delle più incantevoli regioni del circondario di Parigi, tra La Roche Guyon e Vétheuil. Già gli impressionisti furono attratti ed ispirati dalla bellezza del paesaggio. Qui visse e lavorò, creandovi importanti opere, Claude Monet, che riscoprì sotto una luce sempre nuova luoghi e cose come Vétheuil, la riva della Senna e le amate ninfee nel giardino della propria casa di Giverny. L'Île de Chantemesle è un parco di quattro ettari con magnifici alberi. Due spaziose ville sono situate tra le siepi di rododendro in fiore: una è a disposizione degli abitanti, mentre l'altra ospita il personale di servizio.

France
Île Illiec

The Bretonic Île Illiec is a veritable gem of an island, enclosed by the pink rocks typical of the area and covered in magnificent stone pine trees. It once belonged to legendary pilot Charles Lindbergh, who resided on the island with his family from 1936 to 1939. In 1927, the former air mail pilot was the first to fly the 3,418-mile nonstop flight from New York to Paris. It took him 33 hours and 28 minutes to cross the Atlantic in his tiny airplane made of wood and canvas. Lindbergh, who later also purchased Gooch Island in Canada, spent the final years of his life on the island of Maui that belongs to Hawaii. He died on that island in the year 1974, aged 72. Today Île Illiec belongs to the Charles Heidsieck family of the famous champagne dynasty.

Die bretonische Île Illiec ist ein wahres Insel-Kleinod, eingefasst von den für die Region typischen rosafarbenen Felsen und mit prächtigen Pinien bewachsen. Einst gehörte sie der Piloten-Legende Charles Lindbergh, der dort mit seiner Familie von 1936 bis 1939 lebte. Der ehemalige Postflieger vollbrachte 1927 den ersten, 5500 Kilometer langen Nonstop-Flug von New York nach Paris – 33 Stunden und 28 Minuten brauchte er in seinem winzigen Flugzeug aus Holz und Segeltuch, um den Atlantik zu überqueren. Lindbergh, der später auch Gooch Island in Kanada erwarb, verbrachte seine letzten Lebensjahre auf der zu Hawaii gehörigen Insel Maui. Dort starb er 1974 im Alter von 72 Jahren. Heute besitzt die Familie Charles Heidsieck aus der berühmten Champagner-Dynastie die Île Illiec.

L'île bretonne Illiec, est un véritable joyau bordé de falaises roses propres à la région et couvert de pins parasols. Elle a autrefois appartenu au légendaire pilote d'avion, Charles Lindbergh qui y vécut avec sa famille entre 1936 et 1939. En 1927, l'ancien pilote de l'Aéropostale traversa pour la première fois l'Atlantique, soit 5 500 kilomètres, au cours d'un vol en solitaire sans escale reliant New York à Paris. Il effectua ce vol en 33 heures et 28 minutes sur un minuscule avion construit en bois et en toile. Plus tard, Lindbergh acheta aussi Gooch Island au Canada et vécut ses dernières années sur l'île Maui qui fait partie d'Hawaï. C'est là qu'il mourut en 1974 à l'âge de 72 ans. Aujourd'hui, la famille Heidsieck de la célèbre dynastie du champagne est propriétaire de l'île Illiec.

La isla bretona Illiec es una auténtica joya, engarzada por los acantilados rosados que caracterizan la región y con exuberantes pinares. En el pasado, perteneció al legendario piloto Charles Lindbergh, quien residió allí con su familia de 1936 a 1939. El antiguo piloto correo realizó, en 1927, el primer vuelo de 5500 kilómetros sin escalas de Nueva York a París: le llevó 33 horas y 28 minutos cruzar el Atlántico en su minúsculo avión de madera y lona. Lindbergh, quien más tarde también adquirió la isla de Gooch, Canadá, pasó sus últimos años de vida en la isla hawaiana de Maui. Allí falleció en 1974, a los 72 años de edad. En la actualidad, Île Illiec pertenece a la familia Charles Heidsieck, de la renombrada dinastía de Champagne.

L'Île Illiec, in Bretagna, è un vero gioiello incastonato negli scogli rosati tipici della regione e ricoperta di magnifici alberi di pino. Una volta era di proprietà di Charles Lindbergh, il leggendario pilota, che vi abitò con la famiglia dal 1936 al 1939. Nel 1927 l'ex postino volante compì il primo volo non-stop di 5500 chilometri da New York a Parigi, impiegando 33 ore e 28 minuti per sorvolare l'Atlantico con il suo minuscolo aereo di tela e legno. Lindbergh, che in seguito acquistò anche Gooch Island in Canada, trascorse gli ultimi anni della sua vita nell'isola hawaiana di Maui, dove morì nel 1974 all'età di 72 anni. Oggi l'Île Illiec è di proprietà della famiglia di Charles Heidsieck, la celebre dinastia di produttori di champagne.

France
Île Verte

On Île Verte, the water tower of the abandoned village resembles a fortress. Until the mid 20th century it supplied 1,200 people with drinking water—the island's lord had commissioned the village to be built, including a church, school and railway, for his workers and their families. The 1,112-acre island is one of Europe's biggest private islands. Idyllically located in the middle of Garonne river in the Gironde region, which is famous for its wine, the sandy soil on the "Green Island" is the especially suitable for wine to thrive. The mild climate contributes to the first-class red wine produced by the island's exemplary winery. On the mainland across from the island lies the well-known Château Margaux with France's biggest golf course, which contains two 18-hole golf courses.

Wie ein Burgfried wirkt der Wasserturm des verlassenen Dorfes auf der Île Verte. Bis in die Mitte des 20. Jahrhunderts versorgte er 1200 Menschen mit Trinkwasser – der Inselgutsherr hatte für seine Angestellten und deren Familien ein eigenes Dorf errichten lassen samt Kirche, Schule und Eisenbahn. Die Insel umfasst 450 Hektar Land und ist eine der größten Privatinseln Europas. Sie liegt idyllisch inmitten des Flusses Garonne in der Region Gironde. Diese ist berühmt für ihren Wein – auch auf der „Grünen Insel" findet sich der besondere Sandgrund, in dem die Weinpflanzen so gut gedeihen. Das milde Klima trägt zu dem erstklassigen Rotwein bei, den das vorbildlich geführte Inselweingut erzeugt. Auf dem Festland gegenüber der Insel liegt das bekannte Château Margaux mit dem größten Golfplatz Frankreichs. Er verfügt über zwei 18-Loch-Bahnen.

Le château d'eau du village déserté de l'île Verte ressemble à un donjon. Il alimente 1 200 personnes en eau jusqu'à la fin de la première moitié du XXᵉ siècle. Le propriétaire de l'île avait fait construire un village avec une église, une école et une gare pour ses employés et leurs familles. La superficie de l'endroit est de 450 hectares. C'est l'une des plus grandes îles européennes. Elle est située au beau milieu de la Garonne dans la région de la Gironde. Cette dernière est réputée pour son vin. L'île Verte offre également ce sol sablonneux si particulier propice à l'épanouissement des vignes. Le climat doux permet aussi au domaine viticole géré de manière exemplaire de produire un vin de grande qualité. Sur le continent, Château Margaux fait face à l'île avec le plus grand terrain de golf de France : il compte deux parcours de 18 trous.

La torre de agua del pueblo abandonado en Île Verte se asemeja a la torre del homenaje. Hasta mediados del siglo XX este depósito abastecía a 1.200 personas de agua potable; el propietario de la isla construyó para sus empleados y sus familias un pueblo con iglesia, un colegio y una estación. Con su superficie de 450 hectáreas es una de las mayores islas privadas de Europa. Está idílicamente ubicada en medio del río Garonne, en la región de Gironde, famosa por sus vinos; también en esta "isla verde" encontramos el suelo arenoso excelente para el cultivo de las vides. El clima cálido contribuye a la elaboración de un vino tinto de primera, producido en una explotación vinícola gestionada de una forma ejemplar. En tierra firme, en frente de la isla, se levanta el conocido Château Margaux con el mayor campo de golf de Francia. Posee dos pistas de golf con 18 hoyos cada una.

La torre piezometrica del villaggio abbandonato si erge sull'Île Verte come un battifredo. Fino alla metà del XX° secolo essa è servita a procurare acqua potabile a 1200 persone: il proprietario dell'isola aveva fatto costruire per i suoi dipendenti e per le loro famiglie un vero e proprio villaggio provvisto di chiesa, scuola e ferrovia. L'isola, una delle isole private più vaste d'Europa, comprende 450 ettari di terreno. È situata in posizione idilliaca al centro del fiume Garonna, nella regione della Gironda, nota zona vinicola. Anche sull' "Isola verde" si trova quel terreno sabbioso particolarmente adatto alla coltivazione della vite. Grazie alla mitezza del clima, il vigneto dell'isola, curato con grande perizia, produce un ottimo vino rosso. Sulla terraferma, di fronte all'isola, si trova il celebre Château Margaux, con il campo da golf più grande della Francia, provvisto di due piste a 18 buche.

France

Costaérèz

Henryk Sienkiewicz

In the year 1893, the Polish mathematician, inventor and engineer Bruno Abakanowicz erected the picturesque castle on the Breton island of Costaérèz, one of Europe's most beautiful islands. This was where Abakanowicz' close friend, the Polish writer Henryk Sienkiewicz wrote his historical novel "Quo Vadis", for which he was awarded the Nobel price for literature in the year 1905. The castle contains a magnificently decorated knight's hall and a gallery where ballad mongers used to perform in former times.

Auf der bretonischen Insel Costaérèz, eine der schönsten Inseln Europas, erbaute der polnische Mathematiker, Erfinder und Ingenieur Bruno Abakanowicz im Jahr 1893 das pittoreske Schloss. Dort schrieb Abakanowicz' enger Freund, der polnische Schriftsteller Henryk Sienkiewicz, seinen historischen Roman „Quo Vadis", für den er im Jahr 1905 mit dem Nobelpreis für Literatur ausgezeichnet wurde. In dem Schloss finden sich eine prachtvoll dekorierte Ritterhalle und eine Galerie, auf der in vergangenen Zeiten Bänkelsänger auftraten.

Sur la Costaérèz bretonne qui est l'une des plus belles îles d'Europe, le mathématicien, inventeur et ingénieur polonais, Bruno Abakanowicz, a construit en 1893 un château pittoresque. C'est là que son très proche ami, l'écrivain polonais Henryk Sienkiewicz, rédigea son roman historique « Quo Vadis » auquel fut décerné le prix Nobel de Littérature en 1905. Le château abrite une salle des chevaliers décorée avec faste et une galerie accueillant autrefois les chanteurs des rues.

En la isla bretona Costaérèz, una de las más bellas de Europa, el matemático, inventor e ingeniero polaco Bruno Abakanowicz encargó construir el pintoresco castillo en el año 1893. Allí, el escritor polaco Henryk Sienkiewicz, íntimo amigo de Abakanowicz, escribió su novela histórica "Quo Vadis", por el que en 1905 fue distinguido con el Premio Nobel de Literatura. En el castillo puede verse una sala de caballeros decorada suntuosamente y una galería en la que en tiempos pasados cantaban copleros medievales.

Sull'isola bretone di Costaérèz, una delle più belle d'Europa, il matematico, inventore ed ingegnere polacco Bruno Abakanowicz ha costruito nel 1893 il pittoresco castello. Qui lo scrittore polacco Henryk Sienkiewicz, caro amico di Abakanowicz, scrisse il romanzo storico "Quo Vadis", per il quale nel 1905 fu insignito del premio Nobel per la letteratura. Il castello racchiude la sala dei Cavalieri, splendidamente decorata, ed una galleria su cui, in passato, si esibivano i cantastorie.

Great Britain, Channel Islands
Île Brecqhou

The twin brothers Sir David and Sir Frederick Barclay are shy persons, yet very successful publishers of publications such as the "Daily Telegraph", as well as owners of the noble London Ritz Hotel. In 1993, they purchased the precipitous Île Brecqhou to the west of the smallest Channel Island of Sark. This is where the brothers enjoy their highly cherished seclusion—and the tax benefits of the Channel Islands. They invested part of their wealth, estimated at 1.3 billion British pounds, in the erection of a gothic-style castle, rising more than 230 feet above the sea on the rocky island. The Barclays value their privacy above all else. This is why, during the three-year building phase, the construction site was covered with a giant sail. The 1,000 workers involved were sworn to secrecy.

Die Zwillingsbrüder Sir David und Sir Frederick Barclay sind scheue Zeitgenossen, doch höchst erfolgreiche Verleger, unter anderem des „Daily Telegraph", sowie Eigentümer des Londoner Edelhotels Ritz. 1993 erwarben sie die schroffe Île Brecqhou westlich der kleinsten Kanalinsel Sark. Hier genießen die Brüder die ersehnte Abgeschiedenheit – und die steuerlichen Vorteile der Kanalinseln. Einen Teil ihres auf 1,3 Milliarden Pfund geschätzten Vermögens investierten sie in die Errichtung eines Schlosses im gotischen Stil, das 70 Meter hoch über der See auf der Felseninsel thront. Ihre Privatsphäre geht den Barclays über alles. Während der drei Jahre andauernden Bauarbeiten wurde die Baustelle unter einem riesigen Segel versteckt. Die 1000 beteiligten Arbeiter mussten strengstes Stillschweigen geloben.

Les frères jumeaux, Sir David et Sir Frederick Barclay, sont des contemporains farouches et pourtant des éditeurs à succès, notamment du « Daily Telegraph », ainsi que les propriétaires du Ritz, hôtel de luxe londonien. En 1993, ils ont acheté l'île escarpée de Brecqhou, située à l'ouest de la plus petite île anglo-normande de Sark. Là, les frères vivent dans une solitude à laquelle ils aspirent ardemment et profitent des avantages fiscaux des îles anglo-normandes. Ils ont investi une partie de leur fortune, évaluée à 1,3 milliards de livres sterling, dans la construction d'un château inspiré du style gothique, qui trône à 70 mètres au-dessus de la mer. Leur sphère privée leur est plus chère que tout. Pendant les trois années qu'ont duré les travaux, le chantier était caché sous une immense toile. Les 1 000 ouvriers qui y ont participé étaient priés de garder le silence sur leur activité.

Los gemelos Sir David y Sir Frederick Barclay son personas realmente recatadas, y también editores de lo más exitosos, entre otros del "Daily Telegraph", además de ser dueños del refinado hotel Ritz de Londres. En 1993 adquirieron el escarpado Île Brecqhou, situado al oeste de Sark, la isla del Canal de la Mancha más pequeña. Aquí, los hermanos disfrutan del retiro tan ansiado –y de las ventajas fiscales que ofrecen las Islas de la Mancha. Invirtieron parte de su fortuna, estimada en 1.300 millones de libras, en la construcción de un castillo de estilo gótico que corona la isla de rocas a 70 metros del nivel del mar. Para los Barclay, la privacidad es algo fundamental. Durante el período de construcción, de tres años de duración, una lona gigantesca tapaba las obras. Los 1000 obreros empleados tuvieron que guardar el silencio más absoluto.

Anche se persone timide, i gemelli Sir David e Sir Frederick Barclay sono editori di successo, ad esempio del "Daily Telegraph", e sono proprietari dell'esclusivo hotel londinese Ritz. Nel 1993 hanno acquistato Île Brecqhou, un'isola dal paesaggio selvaggio, situata a occidente della piccolissima Isola del Canale di Sark. È qui che i fratelli trovano la solitudine tanto cercata – ed i vantaggi fiscali offerti dall'Isola del Canale. Una parte del loro patrimonio, il cui ammontare viene stimato di 1,3 miliardi di sterline, è stata investita nella costruzione di un castello in stile gotico di 70 metri, che si affaccia sul mare dall'alto della scogliera. La privacy è per i Barclay la cosa più importante. Durante i lavori di costruzione, durati tre anni, il cantiere fu nascosto sotto un grandissimo telone. I 1000 operai che vi hanno lavorato sono stati impegnati a mantenere il segreto più assoluto.

Great Britain
Tresco Island

Cacti, date palms, aloe and lilies—the paths of this blooming island are lined by exotic plants. Its 734 acres make it the second largest among the Isles of Scilly before the southwestern coast of Cornwall. Thanks to the influence of the Gulf Stream, Tresco Island features a subtropical climate, turning it into "England's only South Pacific island". There is no rush on Tresco Island, instead the island offers pure sea air, hiking and bike paths, dreamful beach bays with clean water, small stone mounds between indigenous cottages, two ruins of fortresses and the famous monastery gardens near the old Benedictine cloister. The gardens feature a unique collection of figureheads, stemming from ships that sunk before the island. The Isles of Scilly are famous for their impressive purple-red sunsets.

Kakteen, Dattelpalmen, Aloen und Lilien — exotische Pflanzenarten säumen die Wege dieser blühenden Insel, der mit 297 Hektar zweitgrößten der Isles of Scilly vor der Südwestküste von Cornwall. Tresco Island verdankt dem Einfluss des Golfstroms ein subtropisches Klima, welches die Insel zu „Englands einziger Südseeinsel" macht. Hektik gibt es auf Tresco Island nicht, dafür reine Meeresluft, Wander- und Radwege, verträumte Strandbuchten mit sauberem Wasser, kleine Steinwälle zwischen landestypischen Cottages, zwei Burgruinen und die berühmten Abteigärten am alten Benediktinerkloster. In den Gärten ist eine einmalige Sammlung von Galionsfiguren zu sehen, die aus vor der Insel gesunkenen Schiffen stammen. Die Isles of Scilly sind berühmt für ihre eindrucksvollen, violett-roten Sonnenuntergänge.

Des cactus, palmiers, aloès, lys et autres plantes exotiques bordent les chemins de cette île florissante de 297 hectares, la deuxième des Isles of Scilly par ordre de taille, située au large de la côte sud-ouest de Cornouailles. Grâce à l'influence du Gulf Stream, Tresco Island bénéficie d'un climat subtropical qui fait d'elle « la seule île des mers du Sud de l'Angleterre ». Loin de l'agitation stressante, Tresco Island offre l'air pur de la mer, des sentiers de randonnée, des pistes cyclables, des criques idylliques avec une eau propre, des petits murs de pierre entre les cottages typiques, deux ruines de château fort, ainsi que les célèbres jardins de l'ancienne abbaye bénédictine. On peut voir dans les jardins une collection unique de figures de proue provenant des bateaux qui ont sombré devant l'île. Les Isles of Scilly sont renommées pour leurs impressionnants couchers de soleil violet-rouge.

Cactus, palmeras de dátiles, aloes y lirios: las especies vegetales más exóticas ribetean los senderos de esta isla florida que, con 297 hectáreas, es la segunda isla más grande de las Isles of Scilly, en la costa suroeste de Cornualles. Tresco Island disfruta de un clima subtropical gracias a la corriente del Golfo, que la convierte en la "única isla con tiempo del Pacífico de toda Inglaterra". El ajetreo no existe en Tresco: en su lugar, se respira un aire marítimo puro, hay senderos y carriles de bicicleta, románticas bahías con playas y agua cristalina, pequeños muros de piedra que limitan los característicos "cottages", dos ruinas de castillos y los famosos jardines abadengos del antiguo monasterio benedictino. Aquí puede verse una colección única de mascarones de proa, provenientes de los galeones hundidos en la costa de la isla. Las Isles of Scilly son famosas por sus impresionantes puestas de sol de tonos rojizos y violáceos.

Cactus, palme da dattero, aloe e gigli: una vegetazione esotica fiancheggia i sentieri di quest'isola lussureggiante, che con i suoi 297 ettari è la seconda per grandezza delle Isles of Scilly, di fronte alla costa sud-occidentale della Cornovaglia. Grazie alla corrente del Golfo, Tresco Island gode di un clima subtropicale, che la rende l'"unica isola dei mari del sud appartenente all'Inghilterra". A Tresco Island non esiste la fretta, ma solo aria di mare, piste ciclabili e sentieri per escursione, baie idilliache con acqua pulita, piccoli valli di pietra situati tra i tipici cottage, due castelli in rovina ed i famosi giardini dell'abbazia accanto al convento benedettino. Nei giardini si trova una collezione unica di figure di galeoni, provenienti dalle navi affondate davanti all'isola. Le Isles of Scilly sono celebri per gli splendidi tramonti dalle sfumature rosso-violacee.

Ireland
Horse Island

Picturesque Horse Island is located near the southwestern coast of Ireland. It is a favorite retreat for actors, writers, politicians and business leaders who enjoy relaxing far away from the public eye. Even from the whirlpools of the three luxurious cottages made of natural stone guests can enjoy a view of the wide sea, idyllic beaches and the island's very green hills, complete with sea gulls, seals and otters.

Vor der irischen Südwestküste liegt die pittoreske Horse Island. Schauspieler und Literaten, Politiker und Wirtschaftsführer entspannen sich hier gern weitab der Öffentlichkeit. Die drei luxuriösen Natursteincottages bieten selbst vom Whirlpool aus einen Blick über die weite See, die idyllischen Strände und sattgrünen Hügel der Insel, auf Möwen, Seehunde und Otter.

La pittoresque Horse Island est située au large de la côte sud-ouest de l'Irlande. Des comédiens et gens de lettres, des politiciens et des économistes viennent se détendre ici, loin de la vie publique. Même dans le whirlpool, les luxueux cottages en pierre naturelle offrent une vue sur le large, les plages idylliques, les collines d'un vert intense, les mouettes, les phoques et les loutres de l'île.

En la costa del suroeste de Irlanda se encuentra la pintoresca Horse Island. Actores y literatos, políticos y dirigentes económicos optan por relajarse aquí, alejados de la opinión pública. Sus tres lujosas casas de campo de piedra natural ofrecen vistas al ancho mar, a playas idílicas y a las colinas de intenso color verde de la isla, gaviotas, focas y nutrias, incluso desde la propia bañera de hidromasaje.

Davanti alla costa sud occidentale dell'Irlanda si staglia la pittoresca Horse Island. È qui, lontano dal pubblico, che attori e letterati, politici e dirigenti economici, cercano il relax. I tre lussuosi cottage in pietra naturale offrono anche dalla whirlpool la vista sul mare sconfinato, sulle spiagge idilliache e sulle colline smeraldine dell'isola, dove vivono gabbiani, foche e lontre.

Romantically inclined visitors spend the night on the rustic "shipwreck" positioned in a lonely location on a cliff. In the mornings, visitors can take a refreshing bath in the Atlantic, warmed by the Gulf Stream, during which they can watch the dolphins play in the crystal-clear waters.

Friendly neighbors: A maximum of twelve island vacationers share this piece of land sized 158 acres with friendly sheep and one billy goat. Horse Island has wonderful picnic sites where guests can enjoy freshly-caught salmon, sea trout or fresh mussels cooked in wine right at the beach. At all events, very impressive relics of the Celtic culture going back thousands of years are found everywhere on the island.

Romantiker übernachten im rustikalen „Schiffswrack", das einsam auf einem Kliff thront. Morgens erfrischt ein Bad im vom Golfstrom erwärmten Atlantik, bei dem man dem Spiel der Delfine im kristallklaren Wasser zuschauen kann.

Auf gute Nachbarschaft: Mit freundlichen Schafen und einem Ziegenbock teilen sich maximal zwölf Inselurlauber diesen 64 Hektar großen Flecken Erde. Auf Horse Island finden sich wunderschöne Picknickplätze; dort kann man frisch gefangenen Lachs, Meerforellen oder auch frische, noch am Strand in Wein gekochte Muscheln genießen. Beeindruckend sind in jedem Fall die jahrtausendealten Relikte keltischer Besiedlung, die sich überall auf der Insel finden.

Les romantiques passent la nuit dans une « épave de bateau » rustique qui trône, seule, sur la falaise. Le bain matinal dans l'Atlantique réchauffé par le Gulf Stream est rafraîchissant et l'on peut même observer le jeu des dauphins dans l'eau limpide.

En profitant de l'agréable compagnie des moutons et d'un bouc, les vacanciers au nombre maximum de douze se partagent ce grand morceau de terre de 64 hectares. De magnifiques aires de pique-nique sont aménagées sur Horse Island. Là, il est possible de déguster du saumon fraîchement pêché, des truites de mer ou des moules fraîches au vin préparées sur la plage. Des vestiges millénaires impressionnants de la colonisation celte sont visibles un peu partout sur l'île.

Los románticos se alojan en el rústico "buque naufragado" que, solitario, corona una costa escarpada. Por las mañanas, se puede tomar un refrescante baño en aguas del Atlántico templadas por la corriente del Golfo, durante el que se disfruta del espectáculo de baile que ofrecen los delfines en aguas cristalinas.

Una excelente vecindad: con afables ovejas y un macho cabrío, un máximo de doce turistas se reparten este rincón del mundo de 64 hectáreas. En la Horse Island existen maravillosos lugares donde organizar comidas campestres; en ella se puede disfrutar de salmón recién pescado, de reos o de mejillones al vino preparados en plena playa. Lo que siempre impresiona son las reliquias de miles de años de antigüedad de la colonización celta, esparcidas por toda la isla.

Un'idea per i più romantici: il pernottamento nel rustico "relitto" che, solitario, si erge su una falesia. Al mattino, ci si concede un bagno ristoratore nell'Atlantico mitigato dalla corrente del Golfo, mentre si osservano i delfini giocare nelle acque cristalline.

Rapporti di buon vicinato: quest'angolo di terra di 64 ettari è abitato solo da pacifiche pecore, da un caprone e da un massimo di dodici persone. Horse Island offre deliziosi posti per picnic in cui gustare salmone e trote salmonate appena pescati, o frutti di mare freschi cotti nel vino sulla spiaggia. Di sicuro interesse sono i resti millenari degli insediamenti celtici che si trovano numerosi sull'isola.

Ireland
Waterford Castle

The island of Waterford Castle is located at the sunny south-eastern coast of Ireland, between the Wexford and Cork regions, in the middle of the River Suir with its luscious green embankments. It is distinguished by Waterford Castle, which was erected in the 16th century. From the 11th century until the year 1958, the island belonged to the Fitzgerald family; today the estate serves as a splendid castle hotel.

An der sonnenreichen Südostküste Irlands, zwischen den Regionen Wexford und Cork, liegt inmitten des River Suir mit seinen üppig grünen Uferlandschaften die Insel Waterford. Auf ihr thront das Waterford Castle, das im 16. Jahrhundert erbaut wurde. Die Insel war vom 11. Jahrhundert bis ins Jahr 1958 im Besitz der Familie Fitzgerald, heute dient das Anwesen als prächtiges Schlosshotel.

L'île Waterford Castle avec son paysage verdoyant et luxuriant se situe au large de la côte sud-est de l'Irlande, entre les régions de Wexford et de Cork, au beau milieu de la River Suir. Waterford Castle, construit au XVIᵉ siècle, y trône. Entre le XIᵉ siècle et 1958, il appartenait à la famille Fizgerald. Aujourd'hui, il est transformé en hôtel-château fastueux.

En la soleada costa del sureste de Irlanda, entre las regiones de Wexford y Cork, reposa la isla de Waterford, en aguas del River Suir, con sus exuberantes y verdes paisajes costeros. La corona el Waterford Castle, construido en el siglo XVI. Desde el siglo XI hasta 1958 la isla perteneció a la familia Fitzgerald; actualmente, es un hotel magnífico.

Sulla soleggiata costa meridionale dell'Irlanda, tra le regioni Wexford e Cork, tra le rive verdeggianti del River Suir, è situata l'isola di Waterford Castle, dominata dall' omonimo castello, costruito nel XVI° secolo. Dall'XI° secolo fino al 1958 l'isola è stata di proprietà della famiglia Fitzgerald; oggi il castello è un magnifico hotel.

The impressive interior, the understated atmosphere and the exquisite and unobtrusive service of the castle hotel with its 19 rooms allow visitors to completely relax. Waterford Castle offers services of the highest class and is one of the few deluxe hotels located in south-eastern Ireland. The castle has its own 18-hole golf course surrounded by extensive forests and the River Suir.

Das imposante Interieur, die dezente Atmosphäre und der exquisite, unaufdringliche Service des Schlosshotels mit seinen 19 Zimmern laden zum Entspannen ein. Waterford Castle genügt höchsten Ansprüchen und ist eines der wenigen Deluxe-Hotels in Irlands Südosten. Zum Schloss gehört ein eigener 18-Loch-Golfplatz, umgeben von ausgedehnten Wäldern und dem River Suir.

L'intérieur imposant, la douce atmosphère et le service raffiné et discret de l'hôtel avec ses 19 chambres invitent à la détente. Le Waterford Castle répond aux plus grandes exigences. C'est l'un des rares hôtels de luxe situé dans le sud-est de l'Irlande. Le château offre également un terrain de golf de 18 trous, entouré de forêts étendues et de la River Suir.

Su interior de lo más imponente, el ambiente discreto y el servicio exquisito y reservado del hotel castillo de 19 habitaciones invitan a la relajación. El castillo de Waterford satisface las más altas exigencias y es uno de los pocos hoteles de lujo del sureste de Irlanda. El castillo posee su propio campo de golf de 18 hoyos, rodeado de amplios bosques y por el River Suir.

I sontuosi interni, l'atmosfera sobria ed il servizio squisito e discreto dell'hotel-castello, con le sue 19 camere, invitano al relax. Waterford Castle è in grado di soddisfare tutte le esigenze ed è uno dei pochi hotel de luxe dell'Irlanda sud-orientale. Il castello dispone di un proprio campo da golf a 18 buche, circondato da vasti boschi e dal River Suir.

Scotland
Eilean Righ

Located before the west coast of Scotland, the 212-acre hilly Hebrides island of Eilean Righ appears richly green and majestic when seen from the air and a stroll across it also enchants visitors with its expansive meadows, wild goats and a blooming flora. The name Eilean Righ is Gaelic and means "Royal Island" . It contains the remnants of two fortresses dating from the Iron Age. In the 1930's the island belonged to Sir Reginald Johnston (1874-1938), the teacher of the last Chinese emperor Pu Yi, who even constructed a Buddhist temple on the island. Eilean Righ is the largest island of the Loch Craignish region and belongs to the Scottish earldom of Argyll and Bute.

Sattgrün und majestätisch zeigt sich die 86 Hektar große hügelige Hebrideninsel Eilean Righ vor der Westküste Schottlands aus der Vogelperspektive – und verzaubert auch bei einem Landspaziergang mit ihren weiten Weiden, wilden Ziegen und einer blühenden Pflanzenwelt. Der Name Eilean Righ ist gälisch und bedeutet „Königliche Insel". Hier finden sich die Überreste zweier Festungen aus der Eisenzeit. In den dreißiger Jahren des 20. Jahrhunderts war die Insel im Besitz von Sir Reginald Johnston (1874-1938), dem Lehrer des letzten chinesischen Kaisers Pu Yi, der hier sogar einen buddhistischen Tempel errichten ließ. Eilean Righ ist die größte Insel im Loch Craignish und gehört zur schottischen Grafschaft Argyll and Bute.

À vol d'oiseau, on aperçoit la majestueuse île Hébride aux collines verdoyantes, Eilean Righ, qui s'étend sur 86 hectares au large de la côte ouest de l'Écosse. Elle offre la possibilité de promenades charmantes dans la campagne au milieu de ses grands pâturages, des chèvres sauvages et de plantes florissantes. Le nom, Eilan Righ, signifie « île royale » en gaélique. Là se trouvent les vestiges de deux forteresses de l'Âge du fer. Dans les années 1930, l'île était en possession de Sir Reginald Johnston (1874-1938), professeur du dernier empereur chinois, Pu Yi, qui y fit même construire un temple bouddhiste. Eilean Righ est la plus grande île du Loch Craignish et fait partie du comté d'Argyll et Bute.

A vista de pájaro, la montañosa Isla Hébrida Eilean Righ, de 86 hectáreas de superficie, se presenta verde y majestuosa frente a la costa oeste de Escocia, y fascina, también al pasear por ella, con sus prados, cabras salvajes y una flora exuberante. Eilean Righ es un nombre gaélico y significa "Isla Real". En ella pueden contemplarse las ruinas de dos fortalezas de la Edad del Hierro. En los años treinta del siglo XX, la isla fue propiedad de Sir Reginald Johnston (1874-1938), maestro del último emperador chino Pu Yi, quien incluso hizo construir un templo budista en la isla. Eilean Righ es la mayor isla del lago Craignish y se encuentra en el condado escocés de Argyll and Bute.

L'isola delle Ebridi Eilean Righ, di 86 ettari, di fronte alla costa occidentale della Scozia, si mostra dall'alto verdissima e maestosa. È tuttavia incantevole anche durante una passeggiata, con i suoi vasti pascoli, le capre selvatiche e la vegetazione in fiore. Il nome Eilean Righ è gaelico e significa "isola reale". Vi si trovano i resti di due fortezze dell'età del ferro. Negli anni trenta del XX° secolo l'isola apparteneva a Sir Reginald Johnston (1874-1938), precettore dell'ultimo imperatore cinese Pu Yi, che fece costruire qui addirittura un tempio buddista. Eilean Righ è l'isola più grande di Loch Craignish e fa parte della contea scozzese di Argyll e Bute.

Nature's Masterpieces:
The Emergence of Islands

In the early dawn hours of November 14, 1963 the fishers outside Iceland's southern coast held their breath, interrupted their work and stared across the icy sea. The water was boiling and spluttering, spitting out lava, as ash columns rose from the waves to the sky. The land and sea battled for five days until, amidst great detonations, a volcanic crater arose—an island was born. The new land was christened Surtsey, after Surtur, the mighty fire giant of Norse mythology.

Such dramatic, and from a geological view rapid, island births are extremely rare. Usually such a development requires thousands of years pass to take place. Our planet is constantly subject to change, an unceasing and slow gliding process moves continents by internal earth powers, a process that also contributes significantly to the emergence and disappearance of islands.

Today a total of 500,000 isles of all shapes and sizes rise from the seas, lakes and rivers of our globe. Wherever volcanoes like Surtsey make their way from the depth of the ocean, the sea level drops and reveals new land, where floods isolate headland from coasts or millions of minute polyps create seashores from coral reefs—these are all examples of nature's creation of new islands. There are as many variations in the appearance of islands as there are variations in the mode of their emergence. Islands can consist of atolls surrounded by palms with fine sand beaches, bare rock formations near steep cliffs, or idyllic tree covered hilly landscapes. However, there is one characteristic common to all islands of this earth—each is unique and a true masterpiece of nature.

Geologically, islands are roughly divided into two categories according to their mode of emergence: continental and oceanic islands.

CONTINENTAL ISLANDS

Many of today's isles were once hills rising from spacious flatlands, such as the Seychelles. In the course of millennia the sea level rises and falls, subsequently, islands are born or sink into the deep sea. During the ice age, some 16,000 years ago—geologically speaking almost today—the level of the oceans was around 425 feet lower than today, as large amounts of sea water were trapped on land in the form of ice. Large parts of the continents were dry land, today's straits such as the Bosporus could be crossed by foot and England was no island but part of the European mainland. At the same time, the Bahamas towered as a high coral lime wall over the deep sea basin of the western Atlantic.

When continents collide and sea sediments are pushed on top of each other, underwater mountain ranges are created whose peaks reach out of the water, also creating new continental islands. A prime example of this is the fold mountain range extending from the Peloponnesus via Crete to Anatolia—its larger and smaller peaks extend from the Mediterranean, will one day develop into huge islands and many millennia later be part of a large mountain range between Europe and Africa. Other islands of this type are the Balearics and Cuba. The elongated East Asian islands stretches are evolving in a similar fashion—the oceanic crust of the Pacific is pushed under the continent, sea sediments accumulate and create islands—this is how Japan, among others, emerged.

Additionally, in such active areas of the continental earth crust, volcanoes are created. Sediments from the former sea bed are pushed deep beneath the continents, are heated up until they finally melt and break through the earth crust. Stromboli, located north of Sicily, is such a famous volcanic island.

Continental islands can also be formed from the deposits of silted up matter. For millions of years, the rivers of our earth have carried earth matter from the heart of continents to the edge of the sea—in the river deltas the suspended matter accumulates and new islands emerge. Such river isles are found in the delta of the Nile or in the mouth of the Mississippi, in the Elbe or before Venice.

Right from the start, continental islands have vegetation and are home to their own range of animals and plants.

OCEANIC ISLANDS

These types of islands are either of volcanic origin or coral structures. They emerge from the deep sea far removed from the mainland and are shaped by the climate of the sea and the surf. Their shape can either rise steeply such as Mauritius in the southern Indian Ocean or sunk under the burden of growing coral reefs such as D'Arros in the Amirant group of the Seychelles.

Upon their emergence, volcano islands lack any kind of life, while underneath the coasts of coral islands live only reef creatures and other marine fauna. They remain this way until the wind and the waves carry seeds, eggs and larvae across the open sea as well as land plants and animals to their new habitat. This is why oceanic islands require many years to become a home to its own inhabitants. Oceanic islands are rarely home to amphibians or land mammals. However, they have a large range of birds, insects and various reptiles.

FRINGING REEFS

These reefs develop from continuously growing coral reefs. Examples include the Keys consisting of a multitude of islands in tropical latitudes, the Bahamas and the Great Barrier Reef on the East coast of Australia. Fringing reefs emerge on the shores of oceanic, usually volcanic, islands but also on the edge of continents and their shelves.

Martina Matthiesen / Dipl.-Geologe Firouz Vladi

Kunstwerke der Natur:
die Entstehung von Inseln

Im Morgengrauen des 14. November 1963 hielten die Fischer vor Islands Südküste den Atem an, unterbrachen ihre Arbeit und starrten über die eisige See. Das Meer kochte und tobte und spie ungestüm Lava, Aschesäulen stiegen aus den Wellen in den Himmel auf. Fünf Tage lang kämpften Erde und Meer, bis unter gewaltigen Detonationen ein Vulkankrater ans Tageslicht trat – eine Insel war geboren. Man taufte das neue Land Surtsey, nach Surtur, dem mächtigen Feuerriesen aus der nordischen Mythologie.

Solche dramatischen, geologisch betrachtet rasanten Inselgeburten sind äußerst selten. Meist vergehen für eine solche Entwicklung Jahrtausende. Unser Planet ist in stetem Wandel begriffen, in einem unendlichen und trägen Gleitprozess werden die Kontinente durch innere Erdkräfte verschoben, ein Vorgang, der zum Werden und Vergehen von Inseln erheblich beiträgt.

500 000 Eilande aller Formen und Größen erheben sich heute aus den Meeren, Seen und Flüssen unserer Erde. Wo sich Vulkane wie Surtsey ihren Weg aus der Tiefsee brechen, der Meeresspiegel absinkt und Grund freigibt, wo die Fluten Landvorsprünge von Küsten trennen und Millionen winziger Polypen Korallenriffe zu Ufern aufbauen – überall dort erschafft die Natur neue Inseln. So vielfältig die Entstehungsgeschichte von Inseln ist, so abwechslungsreich ist ihre Erscheinung. Inseln finden ihre Gestalt in palmengesäumten Atollen mit feinem Sandstrand, in kahlen Felsenformationen vor Steilküsten oder auch in idyllisch bewaldeten Hügellandschaften. Eine Eigenschaft jedoch vereint alle Inseln dieser Erde: Jede ist einzigartig und ein wahres Kunstwerk der Natur.

Geologisch unterteilt man Inseln nach ihrer Entstehung grob in zwei übergeordnete Kategorien: kontinentale und ozeanische Inseln.

KONTINENTALE INSELN

Viele heutige Eilande waren einst Hügel, die aus einer weiten Ebene hervorragten, wie beispielsweise die Seychellen. Im Lauf der Jahrtausende steigt oder sinkt der Meeresspiegel, Inseln werden geboren oder versinken in der Tiefe. Während der Eiszeit vor rund 16 000 Jahren – geologisch betrachtet fast noch heute – lag der Spiegel der Weltmeere noch um rund 130 Meter tiefer, große Mengen von Meereswasser waren in Form von Eis auf dem Land gebunden. Weite Teile der Kontinente lagen trocken, heutige Meerengen wie den Bosporus konnte man trockenen Fußes überqueren und England war keine Insel, sondern Teil des europäischen Festlandes. Und die Bahamas ragten derweil als hoher Korallenkalkwall über das Tiefseebecken des Westatlantik.

Wenn Kontinente aufeinander stoßen und Meeresablagerungen sich übereinander schieben, entstehen unterseeisch Gebirge, deren Gipfel aus dem Wasser ragen und so ebenfalls neue kontinentale Inseln bilden. Beispielhaft dafür ist der Faltenbogen, der vom Peloponnes über Kreta bis nach Anatolien verläuft – seine größeren und kleineren Gipfel ragen aus dem Mittelmeer, werden sich eines Tages zu riesigen Inseln entwickeln und viele Jahrtausende später Teil eines großen Gebirges zwischen Europa und Afrika sein. Andere Inseln dieser Art sind die Balearen und Kuba. Ähnlich wachsen die langen Inselgürtel Ostasiens: Die ozeanische Kruste des Pazifik schiebt sich unter den Kontinent, Meeresablagerungen türmen sich auf und bilden Inseln – so entstand unter anderem Japan.

In derart bewegten Regionen der kontinentalen Erdkruste bilden sich zudem Vulkane: Ablagerungen von ehemaligem Meeresboden schieben sich tief unter die Kontinente, heizen sich auf, bis sie schließlich schmelzen und durch die Erdkruste brechen. Eine berühmte Vulkaninsel ist das nördlich von Sizilien gelegene Stromboli.

Kontinentale Inseln können ferner durch Anschwemmung gebildete Aufschüttungen sein. Die Flüsse unserer Erde tragen seit Jahrmillionen von Jahren Erdmassen aus dem Inneren der Kontinente bis an den Rand des Meeres – in den Flussdeltas häufen sich Schwebstoffe auf und neue Inseln entstehen. Solche Flussinseln finden sich im Nildelta oder in der Mündung des Mississippi, in der Elbe oder vor Venedig.

Kontinentale Inseln sind von Anbeginn begrünt und Heimat einer eigenen Tier- und Pflanzenwelt.

OZEANISCHE INSELN

Diese Inseln sind vulkanischen Ursprungs oder Korallenbauten. Sie ragen weit entfernt vom Festland aus der Tiefsee und sind vom Meeresklima und der Brandung geprägt. Ihre Gestalt kann steil aufragend wie Mauritius im südlichen Indischen Ozean sein oder auch unter der Last wachsender Korallenriffe eingesunken wie D'Arros in der Amiranten-Gruppe der Seychellen.

Bei ihrer Entstehung sind Vulkaninseln bar jeglicher Lebenswelt, unter den Küsten der Koralleninseln leben nur Riffbildner und andere marine Faunen. Erst Wind und Wellen befördern Samen, Eier und Larven über das offene Meer – und Landpflanzen und -tiere zu ihrem neuen Lebensraum. Deshalb benötigen ozeanische Eilande viele Jahre, um einem eigenen Inselvolk Heimat zu werden. Auf ozeanischen Inseln finden sich selten eigene Amphibien- oder Landsäugetierarten, hingegen eine Vielfalt an Vögeln und Insekten sowie allerlei Reptilien.

SAUMRIFFE

Solche Riffe aus stetig wachsenden Korallenriffen sind zum Beispiel die mit ihren zahllosen Inseln in tropischen Breiten vertretenen Keys, die Bahamas und das Great Barrier Reef vor der Ostküste Australiens. Saumriffe bilden sich an den Ufern ozeanischer, meist vulkanischer Inseln, aber auch am Rand der Kontinente und ihrer Schelfe.

Martina Matthiesen / Dipl.-Geologe Firouz Vladi

Une oeuvre d'art de al nature :
la naissance des îles

Dans la grisaille matinale du 14 novembre 1963, les pêcheurs de la côte sud de l'Islande retinrent leur souffle, interrompirent leur travail et regardèrent fixement au-delà de la mer de glace. La mer bouillonnait, se déchaînait et crachait de la lave avec fougue ; des colonnes de cendre s'élevaient vers le ciel au-dessus des vagues. Pendant cinq jours, terre et mer se livrèrent un combat sans merci jusqu'à ce qu'un cratère volcanique apparaisse à la lumière du jour avec de violentes détonations – une île était née. On baptisa cette nouvelle terre du nom de Surtsey, d'après Surtur, le puissant géant gardien du feu de la mythologie nordique.

Du point de vue géologique, ces apparitions dramatiques et vertigineuses sont extrêmement rares. Une telle évolution nécessite généralement plusieurs milliers d'années. Notre planète est en perpétuelle mutation. Les continents sont indéfiniment et lentement déplacés par des forces terrestres internes : un processus qui participe considérablement à l'émersion et à la disparition des îles.

500 000 îlots de toutes formes et tailles se dressent aujourd'hui au-dessus des mers, des lacs et des fleuves de notre terre. Là où les volcans comme Surtsey reviennent des profondeurs, où le niveau de la mer s'affaisse et que le fond apparaît, là où les flots séparent les saillies de terre des côtes et transforment en barrières de corail des millions de minuscules polypes – partout, la nature crée de nouvelles îles. Aussi riche est l'histoire de l'émergence des îles, aussi variée est leur apparition. Les îles naissent dans les atolls bordés de palmiers et de plages de sable fin, dans les formations rocheuses devant les falaises ou bien dans les paysages vallonnés, boisés et idylliques. Pourtant, les îles de la planète ont un point commun : chacune est unique et constitue une véritable œuvre d'art de la nature.

Du point de vue géologique, on classe les îles selon leur émersion en deux grandes catégories : les îles continentales et les îles océaniques.

LES ÎLES CONTINENTALES

De nombreuses îles actuelles étaient autrefois des collines se développant sur une vaste plaine, comme c'est le cas pour les Seychelles. Au fil des millénaires, le niveau de la mer monte ou descend, des îles naissent ou disparaissent dans les profondeurs. Pendant la période glaciaire, il y a 16 000 ans – proche d'aujourd'hui du point de vue géologique – le niveau de la mer était inférieur de 130 mètres environ, et de grandes quantités d'eau de mer étaient reliées à la terre sous forme de glace. De vastes étendues continentales étaient asséchées, certains détroits actuels tels que le Bosphore pouvaient être traversés à pied, et l'Angleterre n'était pas une île mais une partie du continent européen. Les Bahamas se dressaient alors comme un rempart de corail et de calcaire au-dessus du bassin des grands fonds de l'Atlantique occidental.

Quand les continents se heurtent et que les dépôts marins se superposent, des montagnes se forment sous la mer dont le sommet émerge à la surface de l'eau, constituant ainsi de nouvelles îles continentales. C'est le cas, par exemple, de la chaîne plissée en arc qui s'étend du Péloponnèse vers l'Anatolie en passant par la Crète. Ses sommets plus ou moins élevés émergent de la mer Méditerranée et se transformeront un jour en îles gigantesques avant de devenir dans plusieurs millénaires parties prenantes d'une grande chaîne montagneuse entre l'Europe et l'Afrique. Les îles Baléares et celle de Cuba sont comparables. C'est ainsi que se développent les grandes ceintures insulaires de l'Asie orientale : la croûte océanique du Pacifique se déplace sous le continent, les dépôts marins se dressent et forment des îles. Le Japon, par exemple, est né de cette façon.

Dans ces régions mouvantes de la croûte terrestre continentale se forment aussi des volcans : les sédiments des sols marins d'autrefois se déplacent profondément sous les continents, chauffent jusqu'à ce qu'ils fondent finalement et traversent la croûte terrestre. Stromboli est une célèbre île volcanique située au nord de la Sicile.

Les îles continentales peuvent aussi être des entassements résultant des alluvions. Les fleuves de notre terre transportent depuis des millions d'années des masses terreuses depuis l'intérieur des continents jusqu'au bord de la mer. Dans les deltas des fleuves s'accumulent des substances en suspension, et de nouvelles îles apparaissent. De telles îles fluviales se trouvent dans le delta du Nil, à l'embouchure du Mississipi, sur l'Elbe ou devant Venise.

Les îles continentales sont verdoyantes dès l'origine et abritent tout un univers animal et végétal qui leur est propre.

LES ÎLES OCÉANIQUES

Elles sont d'origine volcanique ou résultent de constructions coralliennes. Elles émergent très loin du continent, en haute mer, et sont soumises au climat marin et au ressac. Leur forme peut être dressée comme c'est le cas de l'île Maurice au sud de l'océan indien ou bien enfoncée sous le poids des massifs coralliens qui s'y développent, comme l'illustre D'Arros dans l'archipel des Amarantes aux Seychelles.

Au moment de leur émersion, les îles volcaniques sont dénuées de toute forme de vie. Sous les côtes des îles coralliennes ne vivent que des constructeurs coralliens et autre faune marine. Puis le vent et les vagues acheminent des graines, des œufs et des larves, ainsi que des plantes continentales et des animaux dans leur nouvel espace de vie. Mais il faut attendre de nombreuses années pour que les îles océaniques abritent enfin leur propre population. On y trouve rarement des amphibiens ou des espèces de mammifères. Elles accueillent en revanche une grande diversité d'oiseaux et d'insectes ainsi que tous types de reptiles.

LES RÉCIFS FRANGEANTS

Le récifs proviennent des récifs de corail en perpétuel développement et sont notamment représentés par les nombreuses îles des latitudes tropicales telles que les Keys, les Bahamas et la Grande Barrière de Corail devant la côte-est australienne. Les récifs frangeants se forment sur les rives des îles océaniques, souvent sur les îles volcaniques, mais aussi en bordure des continents et de leurs socles.

Martina Matthiesen / Dipl.-Geologe Firouz Vladi

Obras de arte naturales:
la creación de islas

Al amanecer del 14 de noviembre de 1963, los pescadores de la costa sur de Islandia contuvieron la respiración, dejaron de lado su trabajo y se quedaron absortos mirando al mar helado. Éste ebullicionaba, se alborotaba y escupía lava con ímpetu, y unos pilares de ceniza surgieron de las olas. La tierra y el mar lucharon durante cinco días, hasta que, con violentas detonaciones, un cráter volcánico salió a la luz: había nacido una isla. La nueva tierra fue bautizada como Surtsey en honor a Surtur, el poderoso gigante de fuego de la mitología nórdica.

Este tipo de nacimientos dramáticos, vertiginosos desde el punto de vista geológico, son extremadamente inusitados. Normalmente, estos tipos de desarrollo tienen lugar a lo largo de miles de años. Nuestro planeta está sometido a una evolución permanente y, en un lento proceso de deslizamiento interminable, los continentes son desplazados por las fuerzas interiores de la Tierra que provocan la formación y el fin de diferentes islas.

500000 islas de todo tipo de formas y tamaño se erigen actualmente sobre los mares, lagos y ríos de nuestro planeta. Allí donde los volcanes como Surtsey se abren camino desde las profundidades marinas, donde el nivel del mar baja dejando entrever tierra, donde las mareas separan lenguas de tierra de la costa y millones de minúsculos pólipos van convirtiendo arrecifes de coral en orillas: en todos estos lugares, la naturaleza va creando nuevas islas. La apariencia de las islas es tan variada como lo es la historia de la formación de islas. Las islas van tomando formas diversas convirtiéndose en atolones ribeteados de palmeras con playas de arena fina, en estériles formaciones de rocas situadas a orillas de costas escarpadas o también en paisajes de colinas pobladas de idílicos bosques. Y sin embargo, todas las islas tienen una característica en común: cada una de ellas es única, una auténtica obra de arte de la naturaleza.

Geológicamente, las islas se clasifican en dos categorías generales según su origen: islas continentales y oceánicas.

ISLAS CONTINENTALES

Numerosas islas actuales fueron, en sus orígenes, islotes que sobresalían en una amplia planicie, como por ejemplo las Islas Seychelles. A lo largo de los siglos, el nivel del mar va subiendo o bajando, y las islas van naciendo o sumergiéndose en las profundidades. Durante la época glacial de hace aproximadamente 16000 años —desde el punto de vista geológico casi hoy— el nivel de los mares del mundo todavía era unos 130 metros más profundos que en la actualidad: grandes masas de agua marina estaban unidas a tierra en forma de hielo. Otras regiones continentales estaban secas; así, ciertos estrechos marinos como el Bósforo podían ser cruzados a pie sin mojarse, e Inglaterra no era una isla, sino parte de la tierra firme europea. En aquel entonces, las islas Bahamas se elevaban como un muro calcáreo de coral sobre la cuenca abisal del Atlántico occidental.

Cuando los continentes chocan entre sí y los sedimentos marinos se desplazan superponiéndose nacen montañas submarinas cuyas cúspides sobresalen del agua formando nuevas islas continentales. Un ejemplo de ello es el codo ondulado que comienza en el Peloponeso, recorriendo Creta hasta llegar a Anatolia: sus cumbres mayores e inferiores se elevan por encima del Mediterráneo, algún día llegarán a formar islas enormes y miles de años después formarán parte de una gran cordillera entre Europa y África. Las Baleares y Cuba son otras islas de este tipo. Los largos cinturones de islas del Asia oriental también crecen de forma similar: la corteza oceánica del Pacífico se expande por debajo del continente, los sedimentos marinos se van apilando y forman islas: así surgió, entre otros, Japón.

En este tipo de regiones de gran actividad de corteza terrestre continental también nacen volcanes: los sedimentos de antiguos fondos marinos se van insertando por debajo de los continentes, se van calentando hasta que terminan derritiéndose y salen rompiendo la corteza terrestre. Una famosa isla volcánica es Stromboli, situada al norte de Sicilia.

Las islas continentales también pueden ser acumulaciones formadas mediante sedimentación. Los ríos de nuestro planeta llevan millones de años transportando masas de tierra del interior de los continentes hasta las orillas de los mares: en los deltas fluviales se van apilando partículas suspendidas que crean islas. Este tipo de islas fluviales pueden encontrarse en el delta del Nilo o en la desembocadura del Mississippi, en el río Elba o ante Venecia.

Desde sus orígenes, las islas continentales suelen estar cubiertas de hierba y albergan su propia flora y fauna.

ISLAS OCEÁNICAS

Tienen un origen volcánico o son construcciones coralinas. Así, emergen lejos de la tierra firme, desde las profundidades del océano, y se ven influenciadas por el clima marino y el oleaje. Pueden tener una forma que se eleva escarpadamente, como Mauricio, en el sur del Océano Índico, o también aparecer hundidas por el peso de los arrecifes de coral en constante crecimiento, como D'Arros, en las Islas Almirantes de las Seychelles.

Al nacer, las islas volcánicas no presentan ningún tipo de vida, en las costas de las islas coralinas sólo viven organismos constructores de arrecifes y otras especies de fauna marina. El viento y las olas son los que desplazan semillas, huevas y larvas por el mar abierto —llevando flora y fauna terrestres a su nuevo hábitat. Por ello, las islas oceánicas tardan numerosos años en convertirse en el hogar de una comunidad de seres isleños. Es raro encontrar especies de anfibios o mamíferos terrestres en islas oceánicas; por el contrario, existe una gran variedad de aves e insectos, así como todo tipo de reptiles.

ARRECIFES EN ORLA

Los arrecifes de coral en crecimiento constante son, por ejemplo, los Keys, que pueblan las latitudes tropicales con sus innumerables islas, las Bahamas y la Gran Barrera de Arrecife situada frente a la costa oriental de Australia. Los arrecifes en orla se forman a orillas de islas oceánicas mayoritariamente volcánicas, pero también en los litorales continentales y sus plataformas continentales.

Martina Matthiesen / Dipl.-Geologe Firouz Vladi

Capolavori della natura:
la formazione delle isole

All'alba del 14 novembre 1963 i pescatori della costa meridionale dell'Islanda trattennero il fiato, interruppero il loro lavoro e fissarono lo sguardo sul mare gelato. Il mare si agitava impetuoso, vomitando lava, e colonne di cenere si sollevavano dalle onde verso il cielo. La lotta tra la terra e il mare durò cinque giorni, finché tra terribili boati apparve in superficie il cratere di un vulcano: era nata un'isola. La nuova terra fu chiamata Surtsey, in onore di Surtur, il potente gigante di fuoco della mitologia nordica.

È estremamente raro che un'isola si formi in modo così drammatico e rapido dal punto di vista geologico. Normalmente un episodio del genere dura millenni. Il nostro pianeta è in continua trasformazione: un infinito e lento processo di scorrimento, dovuto a forze interne al globo terrestre, fa scivolare i continenti, attivando un processo che contribuisce in maniera decisiva al nascere ed allo scomparire delle isole.

500000 isole di tutte le forme e dimensioni costellano oggi i mari, i laghi ed i fiumi del nostro pianeta. Quando vulcani come Surtsey irrompono dalle profondità marine, quando il livello del mare si abbassa e lascia affiorare il fondo, quando i flutti tagliano dalle coste lingue di terra e milioni di microscopici polipi trasformano in sponde le barriere coralline, allora la natura crea nuove isole. Il loro aspetto è vario come la storia della loro nascita: esistono atolli orlati di palme e di spiagge dalla sabbia sottile, nude formazioni rocciose di fronte a ripide costiere, paesaggi collinosi e idilliaci coperti di boschi. Ma una caratteristica accomuna tutte le isole del mondo: ognuna di esse è unica, una vera meraviglia della natura.

Dal punto di vista geologico, dopo la loro formazione le isole vengono suddivise in due grandi categorie principali: le isole continentali e le isole oceaniche.

ISOLE CONTINENTALI

Molte delle isole attuali erano in passato delle colline che si ergevano da una vasta pianura, come ad esempio le Seychelles. Nel corso dei millenni il livello del mare si alza o si abbassa, alcune isole affiorano, mentre altre sprofondano negli abissi. Circa 16000 anni fa, durante l'era glaciale – geologicamente parlando, quasi oggi – il livello dei mari era di circa 130 metri più basso: grandi quantità di acqua marina erano attaccate alla terra sotto forma di ghiaccio. Gran parte dei continenti era asciutta, attuali stretti di mare come il Bosforo si potevano attraversare a piedi e l'Inghilterra non era un'isola, bensì una parte della terraferma europea. A quel tempo le Bahamas si sollevarono come un muro corallino e calcareo al di sopra del bacino dell'Atlantico occidentale.

Quando i continenti si scontrano e i sedimenti marini si sovrappongono, sotto il mare si formano montagne la cui vetta fuoriesce dall'acqua formando nuove isole continentali. Ne è un esempio il corrugamento che corre dal Peloponneso a Creta all'Anatolia, le cui vette più alte e più basse fuoriescono dal Mare Mediterraneo: esse diventeranno un giorno delle grandissime isole e – molti millenni più tardi – saranno parte di un'imponente catena montuosa tra l'Europa e l'Africa. Altre isole di questo tipo sono le Baleari e Cuba. Simile è anche la formazione delle lunghe cinture di isole dell'Asia orientale: la crosta oceanica del Pacifico si incunea sotto il continente,

i sedimenti marini si sovrappongono e si formano delle isole – questa è anche l'origine del Giappone.

In regioni così mobili della crosta terrestre continentale si formano anche i vulcani: i sedimenti di quello che una volta era il fondo marino si incuneano in profondità sotto i continenti e si riscaldano finché si sciolgono e fuoriescono spaccando la crosta terrestre. Una famosa isola vulcanica è Stromboli, a nord della Sicilia.

Le isole continentali possono inoltre essere dei rialzamenti del terreno formatisi in seguito ad alluvioni. Da millenni i fiumi trasportano masse di terreno dall'interno dei continenti al mare: sui delta dei fiumi si raccolgono sostanze in sospensione che formano nuove isole. Queste isole fluviali si trovano sul delta del Nilo o alla foce del Mississippi, sull'Elba o di fronte a Venezia.

Le isole continentali si presentano verdeggianti sin dalla loro origine ed ospitano fauna e flora proprie.

ISOLE OCEANICHE

Queste isole sono di origine vulcanica o corallina. Si ergono dalle profondità marine lontano dalla terraferma e sono caratterizzate da clima oceanico e da mare frangente. Possono elevarsi ripide come le Mauritius nell'Oceano Indiano meridionale oppure presentarsi abbassate sotto il peso di barriere coralline in crescita, come D'Arros nel gruppo delle Amiranti alle isole Seychelles.

Al momento della loro formazione le isole vulcaniche sono prive di qualsiasi forma di vita, sotto le coste delle isole coralline vivono solo la fauna delle scogliere ed altre creature marine. Sono il vento e le onde a trasportare semi, uova e larve sopra il mare aperto, e piante e animali terrestri che trovano sull'isola nuovo spazio vitale. Per questo motivo le isole oceaniche necessitano di molti anni per poter ospitare una popolazione propria. Sulle isole oceaniche si trovano raramente anfibi o mammiferi terrestri, sono invece comuni molte specie di uccelli, di insetti e di rettili.

BARRIERE DI FRANGENTE

Queste barriere formate da barriere coralline sempre in crescita sono ad esempio le innumerevoli isole Keys, ai tropici, le Bahamas ed il Great Barrier Reef, di fronte alla costa orientale dell'Australia. Le barriere di frangente si formano dalle sponde di isole oceaniche, per lo più vulcaniche, ma anche lungo i continenti e gli zoccoli continentali.

Martina Matthiesen / Dipl.-Geologe Firouz Vladi

INDIAN OCEAN

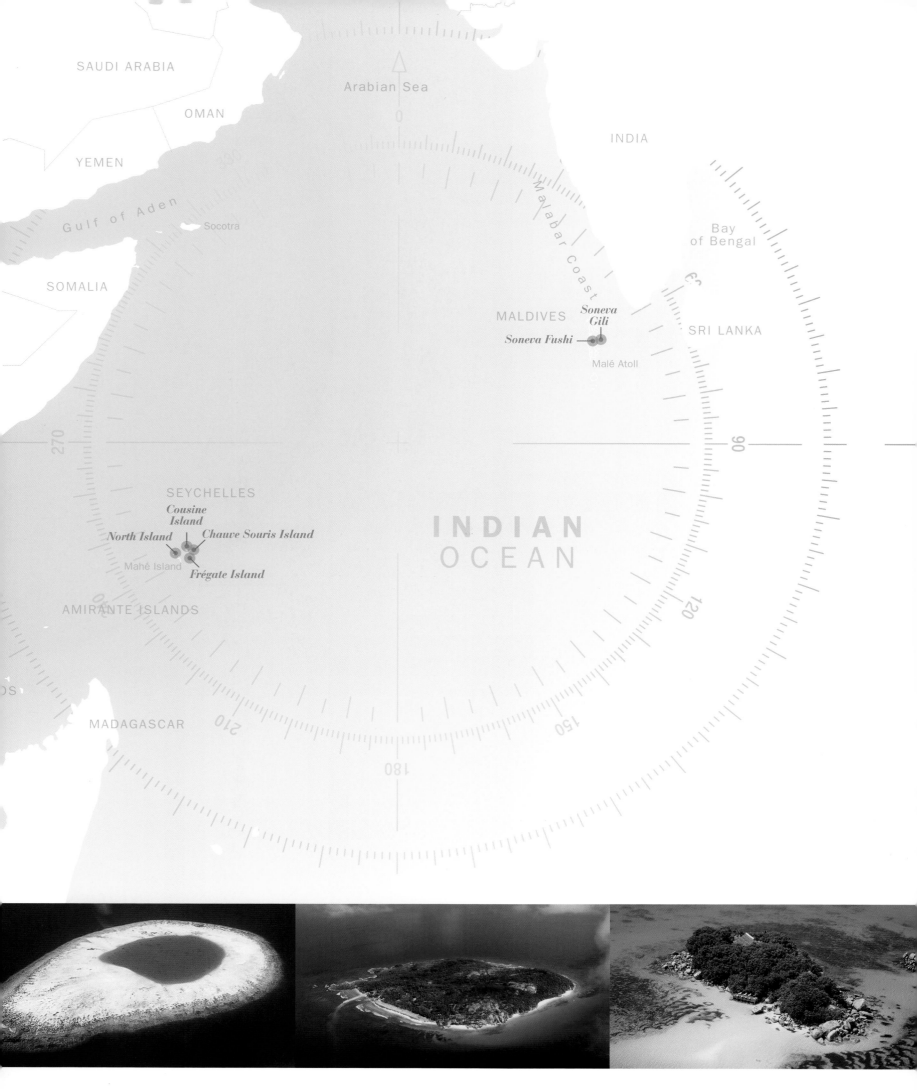

SAUDI ARABIA

OMAN

YEMEN

Gulf of Aden

Socotra

SOMALIA

Arabian Sea

0

Malabar Coast

INDIA

Bay
of Bengal

MALDIVES   *Soneva
Gili*

Soneva Fushi

SRI LANKA

Malé Atoll

270

90

SEYCHELLES

*Cousine
Island*

North Island   *Chauve Souris Island*

Mahé Island

Frégate Island

INDIAN
OCEAN

120

AMIRANTE ISLANDS

210

MADAGASCAR

150

180

Seychelles

Frégate Island

During the last century, Frégate Island served as a vegetable and fruit plantation while today it is smothered in flowers. Its name derives from the rare frigate bird to which it is home. According to the "New York Times", the best beach on the planet is found on Frégate Island.

Frégate Island diente im vergangenen Jahrhundert als Gemüse- und Obstplantage und ist heute über und über bewachsen mit Blumen. Sie ist benannt nach dem seltenen Fregattvogel, der hier lebt. Laut der „New York Times" befindet sich der schönste Strand der Welt auf Frégate Island.

Au siècle dernier, Frégate Island était une plantation d'arbres fruitiers et de légumes. Elle est aujourd'hui couverte de fleurs et porte le nom des frégatidés, oiseaux rares qui vivent ici. D'après le « New York Times » , la plus belle plage du monde est à Frégate Island.

Si en el siglo pasado Frégate Island era una plantación de verdura y fruta, hoy el lugar está inundado de flores. El nombre se lo debe al atípico pájaro Fragata, que habita aquí. Según el "New York Times" en Frégate Island se encuentra la playa más bella del mundo.

Nel secolo scorso vi si coltivavano frutta e verdura: oggi Frégate Island è completamente ricoperta di fiori. Deve il suo nome all'uccello-fregata, una rara specie di uccello marino che vive sull'isola. Secondo il "New York Times" la spiaggia più bella del mondo è quella di Frégate Island.

Many celebrities from the realm of politics, the media and business love the island's isolated bathing bays, its quiet peace and exclusivity, and, most importantly, the private atmosphere of the small island resort on Frégate Island. Many couples who are freshly in love celebrate their wedding in the island's chapel and then spend their honeymoon in the elegant villas on Frégate Island. Brad Pitt and Jennifer Aniston also fell for the charm of this beautiful island that is also known for its free-roaming giant turtles.

Viele Prominente aus Politik, Medien und Wirtschaft lieben die einsamen Badebuchten, den stillen Frieden, die Exklusivität und vor allem die private Atmosphäre des kleinen Insel-Resorts auf Frégate Island. Verliebte Paare feiern ihre Hochzeit in der Inselkapelle und verleben ihre Flitterwochen in den eleganten Villen auf Frégate Island. Auch Brad Pitt und Jennifer Aniston erlagen dem Charme dieser schönen Insel, die auch für ihre frei lebenden Riesenschildkröten bekannt ist.

De nombreuses personnalités éminentes du monde de la politique, des médias et de l'économie apprécient les criques isolées, le caractère paisible, l'exclusivité et par-dessus tout l'atmosphère privée de la petite île de Frégate Island. De nombreux couples d'amoureux viennent célébrer leur mariage dans la chapelle de l'île et passent leur lune de miel dans l'une des élégantes villas de Frégate Island. Brad Pitt et Jennifer Aniston ont également goûté au charme de cette belle île qui est aussi renommée pour ses tortues géantes.

Son muchos los famosos y las personalidades del mundo de la política, los medios de comunicación y las finanzas, que adoran sus bahías solitarias, la serenidad del lugar, la exclusividad, y sobre todo el ambiente de privacidad que se respira en el pequeño resort de Frégate Island. Numerosas parejas de enamorados celebran su boda en la capilla de la isla y disfrutan de la luna de miel en las elegantes villas de Frégate Island. También Brad Pitt y Jennifer Aniston sucumbieron a los encantos de esta hermosa isla, igualmente conocida por la gran cantidad de galápagos que viven en libertad.

Numerose personalità della politica, del giornalismo e dell'economia amano le sue calette solitarie, la pace silenziosa, l'esclusività e soprattutto la privacy del piccolo resort di Frégate Island. Molti innamorati celebrano il loro matrimonio nella cappella dell'isola e trascorrono la luna di miele nelle eleganti ville di Frégate Island. Anche Brad Pitt e Jennifer Aniston sono stati ammaliati dal fascino di questo luogo incantevole noto, tra l'altro, per le tartarughe giganti che vi vivono allo stato libero.

Seychelles
Cousine Island

The small granite Cousine Island is a precious reserve for geckos, turtles and rare birds—the island's proceeds are used for natural protection. The island guarantees undisturbed privacy, as a maximum of eight guests can unwind in four luxury villas, built in the French colonial style, which fit gently into the island's landscape. Sir Paul McCartney and his second wife Heather rented the whole island for their honeymoon and Pierce Brosnan also relaxed with his family on Cousine Island.

Die kleine Granitinsel Cousine Island ist ein kostbares Reservat für Geckos, Schildkröten und seltene Vögel – die Einnahmen des Insel-Resorts kommen dem Naturschutz zugute. Die Insel garantiert eine ungestörte Privatsphäre, maximal acht Gäste erholen sich in vier Luxusvillen im französischen Kolonialstil, die sich sanft in die Insellandschaft einfügen. Sir Paul McCartney und seine zweite Frau Heather mieteten für ihren Honeymoon die gesamte Insel, und auch Pierce Brosnan erholte sich auf Cousine Island mit seiner Familie.

La petite île de granit, Cousine Island, est une réserve précieuse de geckos, de tortues et d'oiseaux rares. Les recettes des hôtels sont reversées au profit de la préservation de la nature. L'île garantit une atmosphère privée non troublée. Un maximum de huit hôtes passent leurs vacances dans quatre villas luxueuses de style colonial français qui s'intègrent harmonieusement au paysage de l'île. Paul McCartney et sa seconde femme Heather ont loué toute l'île pour leur lune de miel. Pierce Brosnan est également venu se reposer sur Cousine Island avec sa famille.

La pequeña isla de granito Cousine Island es una rica reserva de gecos, tortugas y especies raras de aves. El entorno natural saca partido de los ingresos que entran en la isla. El lugar garantiza un ambiente de privacidad, ya que tan sólo ocho huéspedes tienen el privilegio de disfrutar de las cuatro villas de lujo, concebidas en estilo colonial francés, que han sido delicadamente insertadas en el paisaje. Sir Paul McCartney y su segunda mujer Heather alquilaron la isla completa para pasar su luna de miel. También Pierce Brosnan ha disfrutado del relax con su familia en Cousine Island.

Cousine Island, una piccola isola di granito, è una preziosa riserva naturale per gechi, tartarughe ed uccelli rari: i proventi del resort dell'isola sono destinati alla salvaguardia della natura. Cousine Island assicura privacy assoluta: otto ospiti al massimo soggiornano nelle quattro lussuose ville in stile coloniale francese armoniosamente collocate nel paesaggio dell'isola. Sir Paul McCartney e la sua seconda moglie Heather hanno affittato l'intera isola per la loro luna di miele. Anche Pierce Brosnan ha soggiornato qui con la sua famiglia.

Seychelles
North Island

A carefully preserved ecosystem: with great attention to detail and respect towards the preservation of the flora and fauna of this little Seychelles island, renowned architects created a tranquil oasis in the style of an enchanted pirate island. 150 employees look after 22 island guests, who reside in a total of eleven beach chalets. In the houses, that are harmoniously integrated in the lavish and blooming island vegetation, one enjoys all types of luxuries in the midst of nature.

Ein bedachtsam erhaltenes Ökosystem: Mit einem genauen Blick für Details und viel Respekt für den Erhalt der Flora und Fauna dieser kleinen Seychellen-Insel schufen renommierte Architekten eine stille Oase im Stil einer verwunschenen Pirateninsel. 150 Angestellte kümmern sich um 22 Inselgäste, die in insgesamt elf Strand-châlets wohnen. In den Häusern lebt man bei allem Luxus inmitten der Natur, denn sie wurden harmonisch in die üppige und blühende Inselvegetation integriert.

Un écosystème conservé de manière réfléchie : avec un sens du détail et un grand respect de la flore et de la faune de cette petite île des Seychelles, des architectes renommés ont créé ici une oasis paisible dans le style d'une île de pirates enchantée. 150 employés sont en charge des 22 hôtes qui vivent dans les onze chalets situés sur la plage. Les maisons construites au beau milieu de la nature ont été intégrées harmonieusement à la végétation insulaire luxuriante et florissante.

Un ecosistema cuidadosamente conservado: en esta encantadora isla de piratas, afamados arquitectos crearon un oasis tranquilo con una gran sensibilidad por los detalles y mucho respeto por la conservación de la flora y fauna de esta pequeñas isla de las Seychelles. 150 empleados se ocupan de los 22 huéspedes de la isla que viven en once bungaloes. En las casas se vive, a pesar de todo el lujo, en medio de la naturaleza porque en ellas se integró la vegetación exuberante y florida de la isla.

Un ecosistema attentamente protetto: con cura del dettaglio e grande rispetto per la flora e la fauna di questa piccola isola delle Seychelles, rinomati architetti hanno realizzato un'oasi di pace che ricorda una misteriosa isola dei pirati. 150 dipendenti si occupano dei 22 ospiti che abitano gli undici chalet sulla spiaggia. Nelle case, grazie alla perfetta integrazione delle abitazioni nella vegetazione lussureggiante e prosperosa dell'isola, lo stile di vita è un connubio di lusso e natura.

Seychelles

Chauve Souris Island

The small island of dreams Chauve Souris was created by the Italian owner himself—by depositing sand and planting palm trees, his private paradise came into being in the Indian Ocean. In the shade of large trees and luscious tropical vegetation, hidden among the granite rocks typical of the Seychelles, there are two picturesquely designed luxury bungalows covered in palm leaves, as well as a main house including an elegant restaurant.

Die kleine Trauminsel Chauve Souris hat der italienische Eigentümer selbst erschaffen – durch Sandaufschüttungen und Palmenanpflanzungen entstand sein privates Paradies im Indischen Ozean. Im Schatten großer Bäume und üppiger tropischer Vegetation, versteckt zwischen den für die Seychellen typischen Granitfelsen, liegen zwei malerisch gestaltete, mit Palmwedeln gedeckte Luxusbungalows und ein Haupthaus mit einem schönen Restaurant.

Le propriétaire italien de Chauve Souris Island a créé lui-même son île paradisiaque en y déversant du sable et en y plantant des palmiers. Il s'est ainsi offert un paradis privé au beau milieu de l'océan Indien. Les grands arbres et la végétation tropicale abritent du soleil deux pittoresques bungalows luxueux, couverts de frondes de palmiers et une maison principale avec un restaurant raffiné. Ces constructions sont cachées entre les falaises de granit caractéristiques des Seychelles.

La pequeña isla de ensueño Chauve Souris Island ha sido concebida por su propietario italiano, que añadiendo arena y plantando palmeras ha modelado un paraíso en el Océano Índico. A la sombra de imponentes árboles y una exuberante vegetación tropical, escondida entre las típicas rocas de granito de las Seychelles, se levantan dos bungalows de lujo y un edificio central con restaurante, todos ellos exquisitamente decorados.

La piccola, incantevole Chauve Souris Island è stata realizzata personalmente dal suo proprietario italiano: questo paradiso privato nel mezzo dell'Oceano Indiano è stato creato ammucchiando grandi quantità di sabbia e piantando numerose palme. All'ombra di grandi alberi e della lussureggiante vegetazione tropicale, nascosti tra gli scogli di granito tipici delle Seychelles, si trovano due incantevoli e lussuosi bungalow ricoperti di foglie di palma. La casa principale ospita un elegante ristorante.

Maledives, Baa Atoll
Soneva Fushi

A six-star Robinson-style island—those who appreciate natural island life as well as the highest levels of luxury, will fall in love with the island resort of Soneva Fushi whose overriding principle is the conservation of nature.

Eine Sechs-Sterne-Insel im Robinson-Stil — wer sowohl ein naturnahes Inselleben schätzt als auch höchsten Luxus, der wird sein Herz an das Insel-Resort Soneva Fushi verlieren, in dem Naturschutz oberstes Gebot ist.

Une île six étoiles en style Robinson – ceux qui aspirent à la fois à une vie insulaire proche de la nature et au plus grand luxe seront comblés avec le complexe hôtelier Soneva Fushi où la préservation de la nature est l'une des exigences premières.

Una isla de seis estrellas en estilo Robinson –quienes valoren tanto la vida isleña entorno a la naturaleza como el lujo en su máxima expresión, quedaran prendados del resort de Soneva Fushi, lugar donde la protección de la naturaleza es ley de oro.

Un'isola a sei stelle in stile Robinson – chi apprezza sia la vita nella natura, sia il lusso più esclusivo, rimarrà incantato dal resort Soneva Fushi, che propone un soggiorno all'insegna della protezione dell'ambiente.

"Soneva Fushi"—behind the name of the resort is a love story. The Swedish top model Eva Malmström and the British-Indian businessman Sonu Shivdasani fell in love with each other and with the wonderfully peaceful Maldives island of Kunfunadhoo with its dense jungles. 1995 they combined their first names to the melodious name "Soneva" and founded on Kunfunadhoo the six stars resort that won frequent awards. While Sonu Shivdasani is responsible for the management of the resort, his wife Eva takes care of the stylish interior furnishings. Today, resorts in 14 countries belong to the couple's successful hotel group Six Senses Resorts & Spas.

„Soneva Fushi" – hinter dem Namen des Resorts steht eine Liebe: Das schwedische Topmodel Eva Malmström und der britisch-indische Geschäftsmann Sonu Shivdasani verloren ihr Herz aneinander und an die wunderbar friedliche, mit dichtem Dschungel bewachsene Malediven-Insel Kunfunadhoo. 1995 vereinten sie ihre Vornamen zu dem wohlklingenden Namen „Soneva" und gründeten auf Kunfunadhoo das vielfach ausgezeichnete Sechs-Sterne-Resort. Während Sonu Shivdasani für das Management des Resorts verantwortlich ist, obliegt seiner Frau Eva die stilvolle Inneneinrichtung. Heute gehören Resorts in 14 Ländern zu der erfolgreichen Hotelgruppe Six Senses Resorts & Spas des Ehepaares.

Le nom de « Soneva Fushi » dissimule une histoire d'amour : le top-modèle suédois, Eva Malmström et Sonu Shivdasani, homme d'affaire britannique-indien sont tombés amoureux l'un de l'autre ainsi que de la paisible île des Maldives Kunfunadhoo, couverte d'une jungle luxuriante. En 1995, ils ont uni leurs prénoms pour créer celui de « Soneva » aux jolies consonances et ils ont construit sur Kunfunadhoo un resort six étoiles, primé de nombreuses fois. Alors que Sonu Shivdasani est en charge de la direction du resort, sa femme Eva s'occupe de l'aménagement intérieur avec beaucoup de goût. Aujourd'hui, le groupe d'hôtels renommé du couple, Six Senses Resorts & Spas, compte des resorts dans 14 pays différents.

"Soneva Fushi" –detrás del nombre de esta instalación vacacional se esconde un amor: la modelo sueca Eva Malmström y el empresario de origen británico e hindú Sonu Shivdasani además de enamorarse el uno del otro perdieron también el corazón por Kunfunadhoo, esta isla de las Maldivas maravillosamente tranquila y cubierta por una densa jungla. En 1995 unieron sus nombres de pila para crear el agradable nombre "Soneva" y fundaron esta instalación de seis estrellas. Mientras que Sonu Shivdasani es el responsable de la gestión, su esposa Eva se ocupa de decorar con estilo los interiores. Hoy, complejos turísticos en 14 países pertenecen al exitoso grupo hotelero Six Senses Resorts & Spas del matrimonio.

"Soneva Fushi": il nome di questo resort cela un amore: la topmodel svedese Eva Malmström e l'uomo d'affari anglo-britanico Sonu Shivdasani si sono innamorati l'uno dell'altra e di Kunfunadhoo, la tranquilla isola delle Maldive ricoperta dalla giungla. Nel 1995 hanno fuso i loro nomi di battesimo nell'armonioso "Soneva" e hanno realizzato a Kunfunadhoo questo resort a sei stelle già più volte premiato. Mentre Sonu Shivdasani è responsabile

della gestione del resort, sua moglie Eva si occupa del raffinato arredamento. Oggi, diversi resort realizzati in 14 paesi fanno parte dell'affermato gruppo alberghiero Six Senses Resorts & Spas di proprietà della coppia.

An own small world: Soneva Fushi Resorts' luxurious Jungle Reserve contains, on 2033 square yards, a beach villa, an outdoor swimming complex, a tree residential house with a waterslide to the private pool and a spa suite with massage beds, steam bath, rainwater shower, and an air conditioned fitness room. The guests are pampered by three butlers, the exclusive "Mr. Friday Service". This reserve promises undisturbed privacy and maximum relaxation.

Eine eigene kleine Welt: Das luxuriöse Jungle Reserve des Resorts Soneva Fushi umfasst auf 1700 Quadratmetern Fläche eine Strandvilla, eine Badelandschaft unter freiem Himmel, ein Baumwohnhaus mit Wasserrutsche in den Privatpool und eine Spa-Suite mit Massagebetten, Dampfbad, Regendusche und klimatisiertem Fitnessraum. Die Gäste werden von drei Butlern verwöhnt – dem exklusiven „Mr. Friday Service". Dieses Reserve verspricht eine ungestörte Privatsphäre und maximale Erholung.

Un petit univers propre : la luxueuse Jungle Reserve du resort Soneva Fushi comprend sur 1700 mètres carrés une villa située en bord de plage, un paysage balnéaire à ciel ouvert, un petit pavillon dans les arbres avec un toboggan qui accède à la piscine privée et un spa avec des lits pour les massages, un bain de vapeur, une douche de pluie et une salle de fitness climatisée. Les hôtes sont choyés par trois maîtres d'hôtel qui constituent le « Mr. Friday Service ». Cette réserve assure le respect d'une sphère tout à fait privée et un repos maximum.

Un pequeño mundo particular: la lujosa Jungle Reserve del centro de Soneva Fushi ocupa una superficie de 1.700 metros cuadrados que incluyen una villa en la playa, un balneario a cielo abierto, una casa en un árbol con tobogán de agua en la piscina privada y una suite de spa con camas de masages, baño de vapor, una ducha de lluvia y un estudio de deporte climatizado. Los huéspedes son mimados por tres mayordomos –el exclusivo "Mr. Friday Service". Esta reserva promete una tranquila esfera privada y descanso absoluto.

Un piccolo mondo a parte: su una superficie di 1700 metri quadrati, la lussuosa Jungle Reserve del resort Soneva Fushi comprende una villa sulla spiaggia, un impianto balneare all'aperto, una casa costruita su un albero con scivolo acquatico nella piscina privata e una suite spa con lettini per i massaggi, bagno turco, doccia tropicale emozionale e palestra climatizzata. Tre maggiordomi – l'esclusivo "Mr. Friday Service", – si occupano degli ospiti. Una reserve che è una promessa di privacy assoluta e completo relax.

Soneva Gili

Elegant stilt buildings over a picturesque lagoon—the guests of Soneva Gilis reside above the sea. Nestled harmoniously among palm trees, the island also includes a restaurant, bar, cleaners, library, kindergarten and even a jeweler.

Elegante Pfahlbauten in einer malerischen Lagune — die Gäste Soneva Gilis wohnen über dem Meer. Auf der Insel befinden sich, harmonisch zwischen Palmen gelegen, Restaurant, Bar, Reinigung, Bücherei, Kindergarten und sogar ein Juwelier.

Des constructions élégantes sur pilotis dans une lagune pittoresque : les hôtes de Soneva Gili vivent sur la mer. L'île abrite aussi, harmonieusement disposés entre les palmiers, un restaurant, un bar, un pressing, une bibliothèque, une garderie d'enfants et même un bijoutier.

Elegantes construcciones de pilotes se erigen sobre una laguna fascinante. De esta forma los huéspedes de Soneva Gili viven sobre el mar. Insertados armoniosamente entre palmeras se ubican restaurante, bar, tintorería, librería, jardín de infancia e incluso una joyería.

Una pittoresca laguna in cui si ergono eleganti palafitte: gli ospiti di Soneva Gili abitano sopra il mare. Sull'isola si trovano, cinti da splendidi palmeti, un ristorante, un bar, una tintoria, una libreria, un asilo infantile e addirittura una gioielleria.

A family or a group of friends of up to eight people can enjoy an exclusive vacation in this very elegantly furnished, meticulously styled, stilt house compound. On 1,674 square yards living space across five separate buildings, it offers an expansive lounge, two sleeping chambers with stunning outdoor bathing areas, a guest-room, a private spa, a sauna, as well as a massage and fitness pavilion. Additional highlights are the carefully stocked wine cellar, a private swimming pool with underwater music, two small motorboats and a waterslide for children.

Eine Familie oder Freundesgruppe von bis zu acht Personen kann einen exklusiven Urlaub in dieser bis in das kleinste Detail perfekt konzipierten und hochelegant ausgestatteten Pfahlbauanlage genießen. Sie bietet auf 1400 Quadratmetern Wohnfläche in fünf separaten Bauten eine weitläufige Lounge, zwei Schlafgemächer mit hinreißenden Outdoor-Badebereichen, ein Gästezimmer, ein privates Spa, eine Sauna sowie einen Massage- und Fitnesspavillon. Weitere Highlights sind der gut sortierte Weinkeller, der private Swimmingpool mit Unterwassermusik, zwei kleine Motorboote und eine Wasserrutsche für Kinder.

Une famille ou bien un groupe d'amis composé de huit personnes au plus peuvent passer des vacances exclusives en profitant de cet aménagement sur pilotis des plus élégants qui a été conçu à la perfection jusque dans ses moindres détails. Il offre une surface habitable de 1 400 mètres carrés avec cinq constructions séparées, un salon immense, deux chambres à coucher avec salles de bain en plein air ravissantes, une chambre d'hôte, un spa privé, un sauna, ainsi qu'un pavillon de massage et de fitness. La cave à vins de qualité offre d'autres surprises, de même que la piscine privée avec musique sous l'eau, les deux petits bateaux à moteur et le toboggan pour les enfants.

Una familia o un grupo de amigos de hasta ocho personas pueden pasar unas exclusivas vacaciones en esta instalación sobre pilotes elegantemente equipada y concebida a la perfección hasta en el más pequeño detalle. En su superficie de 1.400 metros cuadrados ofrece en cinco construcciones separadas un amplio lounge, dos dormitorios con encantadoras zonas de baño en el exterior, una habitación para invitados, un spa privado, una sauna y un pabellón de masaje y de deporte. También destacan la bien aprovisionada bodega, la piscina privada con música debajo del agua, dos pequeñas barcas motoras y un tobogán de agua para los niños.

Una famiglia o un gruppo di amici fino a otto persone possono godere di una vacanza esclusiva in questa struttura su palafitte, elegantissima e realizzata con grande cura fin nei minimi particolari. Su una superficie abitabile di 1400 metri quadrati, in cinque costruzioni separate, sono disponibili una spaziosa lounge, due camere da letto con magnifiche zone bagno outdoor, una camera per gli ospiti, una spa privata, una sauna e un padiglione per massaggi e fitness. Altre attrazioni sono la fornitissima cantina, la piscina privata con musica subacquea, due piccole barche a motore e uno scivolo acquatico per i bambini.

South China
Sea

PHILIPPINES

MALAYSIA

Sumatra

INDONESIA

Java   Bali

PAPUA
NEW GUINEA

Timor

INDIAN
OCEAN

Timor Sea

*Bedarra
Island*

Cairns ∎

AUSTRALIA

Great Barrier Reef

Tasman
Sea

AUSTRALIA, NEW ZEALAND &

SOUTHERN
OCEAN

PACIFIC
OCEAN

FIJI ISLANDS

SAMOA

Motu Tane   *Motu*
            Haapiti   *Tetiaroa*
                        Atoll

Turtle Island   Vanua Levu

Bora Bora

Viti Levu

Tiano
Island   Tahiti

New Caledonia   FRENCH
                                POLYNESIA

NEW ZEALAND

Forsyth Island

Pohuenui Island

SOUTH PACIFIC

Australia
Bedarra Island

Bedarra Island, located near the north coast of Queensland, is the ideal setting for those whose dearest wish is to escape and be far removed from the hustle and bustle of the world. The island's extensively spreading palm trees, hidden bays, extensive sand beaches and tropical vegetation turn holidays spent on Bedarra into an unforgettable experience of nature.

Unauffindbar sein und fern vom hektischen Treiben der Welt – wer sich nichts sehnlicher wünscht als dies, für den ist Bedarra Island an der Nordküste von Queensland die ideale Zufluchtsstätte. Ausladende Palmen, versteckte Buchten, weite Sandstrände und die tropische Vegetation machen Ferientage auf Bedarra zu einem unvergesslichen Naturerlebnis.

Bedarra Island, située sur la côte septentrionale de Queensland, est le refuge idéal pour celui qui n'aspire à rien de plus que d'être introuvable et éloigné de l'agitation stressante du monde. Les palmiers amples, les criques cachées, les immenses plages de sable, de même que la végétation tropicale offrent aux vacanciers une expérience inoubliable.

Estar ilocalizable y alejado del ajetreo del mundo. Para quien no exista mayor deseo que éste, Bedarra Island, ubicada en la costa norte de Queensland, es el refugio ideal. Largas palmeras, bahías escondidas, vastas playas de arena y la vegetación tropical convierten las vacaciones en una inolvidable experiencia en plena naturaleza.

Irreperibili e lontani dalla vita frenetica: Bedarra Island, sulla costa settentrionale del Queensland, è il rifugio ideale per chi non desidera altro che questo. Palme rigogliose, baie nascoste, vaste spiagge sabbiose e vegetazione tropicale fanno delle vacanze a Bedarra un'indimenticabile esperienza alla scoperta della natura.

Diary and organizer are confined to the suitcase as the daily rhythm on Bedarra Island is determined solely by the movement of the sun. The background noise coming from the luscious rainforest, the steady sound of the breakers and the picturesque sunsets help to forget the rest of the world. Two exclusive resorts—Bedarra Bay and Bedarra Hideaway—are stylish havens of relaxation whose luxurious villas fit harmoniously into the gorgeous landscape.

Terminkalender und Organizer müssen im Koffer bleiben, allein der Lauf der Sonne bestimmt den Lebensrhythmus auf Bedarra Island. Die Geräuschkulisse des üppigen Regenwaldes, die stetige Brandung und die malerischen Sonnenuntergänge lassen jeden Gedanken an den Rest der Welt schwinden. Zwei exklusive Resorts – Bedarra Bay und Bedarra Hideaway – bilden stilvolle Erholungsoasen, deren luxuriöse Villen sich harmonisch in die prächtige Landschaft einfügen.

Les agendas et les organisers n'ont pas leur place ici. Seule la course du soleil détermine le rythme de vie sur Bedarra Island. Le bruit de fond de la forêt tropicale luxuriante, l'incessant déferlement des vagues et les couchers de soleil pittoresques empêchent de penser au reste du monde. Deux complexes hôteliers exclusifs – Bedarra Bay et Bedarra Hideaway – constituent des oasis de repos de bon goût et leurs villas luxueuses s'intègrent harmonieusement au paysage somptueux.

Que la agenda se quede en la maleta: en Bedarra Island el ritmo de vida lo determina el sol. El espectáculo de sonidos que ofrece la selva tropical, el continuo romper de las olas y las idílicas puestas de sol difuminan todo pensamiento que tenga que ver con el resto del mundo. Dos resorts exclusivos, Bedarra Bay y Bedarra Hideaway, con sus lujosas villas cargadas de estilo insertadas armónicamente en un paisaje exuberante, constituyen auténticos oasis de placer.

Agenda e organizer devono restare in valigia: solo la posizione del sole segna il ritmo della vita a Bedarra Island. I rumori della lussureggiante foresta tropicale, il continuo infrangersi delle onde ed i pittoreschi tramonti fanno dimenticare completamente il resto del mondo. Due resort esclusivi – Bedarra Bay e Bedarra Hideaway – sono eleganti oasi di riposo con lussuose ville immerse in un paesaggio di sogno.

New Zealand

Forsyth Island

The charm of unspoiled Forsyth Island derives from its enchanted fern forests and scented Manuka tree alleys, awe-inspiring cliffs, as well as secluded beaches. Even in green New Zealand, it represents an unusual natural monument as a home to the Kiwi bird and the indigenous Milk Wood Tree. In the previous century, farmers used the fertile meadows for sheep raising. For the past two decades, however, nature has started to once again repossess the lands. Forsyth Island is located between New Zealand's northern and southern islands in the midst of the Marlborough Sound's impressive world of islands. "Te Paruparu"—The Good. This was the name given to Forsyth Island already by the Maori, the first inhabitants of New Zealand—and to this day visitors find peace and relaxation on this island. The noble "Te Paruparu" lodge, constructed from local wood, lies quietly on a hill with an extensive view across the bays of Marlborough Sound. The 1729-acre island also features 31 miles of winding paths suited for hiking and walking around the island and up the three mountain tops that are almost 1312 feet high.

Verwunschene Farnwälder und duftende Manukabaumalleen, imposante Klippen und einsame Strände bestimmen den Charme der sehr ursprünglichen Forsyth Island. Sie ist selbst für das grüne Neuseeland ein kostbares Naturdenkmal, hier sieht man den Kiwi-Vogel sowie den endemischen „Milk-Wood-Tree". Nachdem im vorigen Jahrhundert Farmer die fruchtbaren Weiden zur Schafzucht nutzten, erobert sich seit zwei Jahrzehnten die Natur das Land zurück. Forsyth Island liegt zwischen der Nord- und der Südinsel Neuseelands, inmitten der imposanten Inselwelt des Marlborough Sound.
„Te Paruparu" – die Gute: Diesen Namen gaben schon die Maori, die Erstbewohner Neuseelands, Forsyth Island – und auch heute findet hier jeder Besucher Frieden und Ruhe. Still liegt die edle, aus heimischen Hölzern errichtete Lodge „Te Paruparu" auf einer Anhöhe mit einem weiten Blick über die Buchten des Marlborough Sound. 50 Kilometer Spazier- und Wanderwege führen in Serpentinen um die 700 Hektar große Insel und hinauf auf die drei fast 400 Meter hohen Berggipfel.

Des forêts enchantées de fougères, des allées de manukas parfumées ainsi que des écueils imposants et des plages isolées caractérisent le charme de la très authentique Forsyth Island. Cette île est un site classé précieux de la verte Nouvelle-Zélande. On peut y voir les oiseaux kiwis ainsi que l'endémique arbre à lait. Après que les fermiers ont au siècle passé consacré les fertiles pâturages à l'élevage des moutons, la nature reprend ici le dessus depuis deux décennies. Forsyth Island est située entre le sud et le nord de l'île de la Nouvelle-Zélande, au beau milieu de l'univers insulaire imposant de Marlborough Sound.
« Te Paruparu » – la bonne : les Maoris qui furent les premiers habitants de la Nouvelle-Zélande baptisèrent ainsi Forsyth Island. Aujourd'hui encore, les visiteurs y trouvent le calme et la sérénité. La paisible demeure,

« Te Paruparu », construite avec le bois des environs se dresse sur une hauteur et offre un vaste aperçu des criques de Marlborough Sound. 50 kilomètres de sentiers de randonnée serpentent parmi les 700 hectares de la grande île et grimpent au sommet de la montagne qui atteint presque les 400 mètres.

Hechizantes bosques de helechos y aromáticas avenidas de árboles Manuda, impresionantes riscos y solitarias playas crean el encanto de la prístina Forsyth Island. Esta isla es, incluso para la verde Nueva Zelanda, un valioso monumento de la naturaleza; aquí puede observarse al pájaro kiwi y al endémico "Milk Wood Tree". Después de que en el último siglo los granjeros emplearan las fértiles praderas para el pasto de las ovejas, desde hace dos décadas la naturaleza reconquista nuevamente la tierra. Forsyth Island está situada entre las islas Norte y Sur de Nueva Zelanda, en medio del imponente mundo de islas del Marlborough Sound.
"Te Paruparu" –la buena: este nombre se lo dieron a Forsyth Island los maori, los primeros habitantes de Nueva Zelanda, y aún hoy los visitantes encuentran aquí paz y tranquilidad. El elegante pabellón "Te Paruparu", construido con maderas autóctonas, está situado en un lugar tranquilo y elevado y disfruta de una amplia vista sobre las calas del Marlborough Sound. 50 kilómetros de serpenteantes caminos para pasear y hacer excursiones recorren esta isla de 700 hectáreas y llevan hasta la cumbre de la montaña, de casi 400 metros de altitud.

Foreste incantate di felci e viali di manuka profumata, imponenti scogliere e spiagge solitarie costituiscono il fascino primitivo di Forsyth Island, preziosa riserva naturale anche per la verde Nuova Zelanda e patria dell'uccello kiwi e dell'albero milkwood, qui assai diffuso. Dopo lo sfruttamento dei fertili pascoli da parte dei contadini, che nel secolo scorso li hanno utilizzati per l'allevamento degli ovini, ormai da due decenni la natura sta riconquistando il paese. Forsyth Island è situata tra l'isola settentrionale e quella meridionale della Nuova Zelanda, al centro del vasto arcipelago Marlborough Sound.
"Te Paruparu", la buona: già i Maori, i primi abitanti della Nuova Zelanda, chiamarono così Forsyth Island – ancora oggi, chi la visita vi trova pace e tranquillità. L'elegante lodge "Te Paruparu", costruito con legni locali, è situato in posizione discreta su un'altura da cui si gode la libera vista delle insenature di Marlborough Sound. 50 chilometri di sentieri per escursioni e passeggiate si snodano attraverso i 700 ettari dell'isola, inerpicandosi verso le tre cime montuose fino ad un'altitudine di quasi 400 metri.

New Zealand
Pohuenui Island

From the air, Pohuenui Island looks like a part of the Alps that has fallen into the Pacific. Located within Marlborough Sound, New Zealand's sunniest region, Pohuenui measures about 5,190 acres—ten times the size of Monaco—making it one of the largest private islands in the South Pacific. It includes 31 miles of coastline with numerous beach bays, while more than 28 miles of farm roads and natural roads cross the indigenous pastures and hilly landscapes. Rising about 1,970 feet above the sea, the island's peak offers a fantastic panoramic view across Marlborough Sound and the neighboring islands. The wild green mountainous regions with their diverse flora and fauna, as well as the sea with its multitude of fishes, dolphins, seals and whales, are a special thrill for nature-loving visitors. With a bit of luck one can catch sight of one of the island's rare penguins, but visitors are sure to encounter at least one of the 3,500 sheep residing on the island.

Als wäre ein Teil der Alpen in den Pazifik gefallen, so wirkt Pohuenui Island aus der Luft. In der sonnigsten Region Neuseelands, im Marlborough Sound, gelegen, ist Pohuenui mit über 2100 Hektar Fläche – zehnmal mehr als das Fürstentum Monaco – eine der größten Privatinseln im Südpazifik. Sie umfasst 50 Kilometer Küstenlinie mit zahlreichen Strandbuchten, mehr als 45 Kilometer Farmwege und Naturstraßen führen durch das ursprüngliche Weide- und Hügelland. Der 600 Meter hohe Inselgipfel bietet einen phantastischen Panoramablick über den Marlborough Sound und die benachbarten Inseln. Die grüne, wilde Berglandschaft mit ihrer artenreichen Flora und Fauna sowie das Meer mit seinem Fischreichtum, den Delfinen, Seehunden und Walen lassen die Herzen naturverbundener Besucher höher

schlagen. Mit ein wenig Glück kann man hier einen der seltenen Pinguine zu Gesicht bekommen, auf jeden Fall wird der Gast aber einem der 3500 Schafe begegnen, die auf der Insel leben.

Vue d'en haut, Pohuenui Island ressemble à une partie des Alpes qui serait tombée dans le Pacifique. L'île se situe à Marlborough Sound, la région la plus ensoleillée de la Nouvelle-Zélande. Elle s'étend sur plus de 2 100 hectares de superficie – soit dix fois la Principauté de Monaco. C'est l'une des plus grandes îles privées du Pacifique Sud. Sa côte de 50 kilomètres de long comprend de nombreuses criques. Plus de 45 kilomètres de chemins de ferme et de routes naturelles sillonnent ce paysage de pâturages et de collines. Le sommet de l'île d'une hauteur de 600 mètres offre un panorama fantastique sur Marlborough Sound et sur les îles voisines. Ce paysage montagneux verdoyant et à l'état sauvage qui accueille de nombreuses espèces de faune et de flore, ainsi que la mer avec sa variété de poissons, ses dauphins, ses phoques et ses baleines font battre plus vite le cœur des amoureux de la nature. Avec un peu de chance, il est possible de voir surgir l'un des rares pingouins, mais quoiqu'il en soit, le visiteur verra de toute façon l'un des 3 500 moutons qui vivent sur l'île.

Vista desde el cielo, Pohuenui Island se levanta como si de un pedazo de los Alpes caído en el mar se tratase. Está ubicada en la región más soleada de Nueva Zelanda, en Marlborough Sound, y constituye, con sus 2100 hectáreas, una superficie diez veces mayor que el Principado de Mónaco, lo que la convierte en una de las mayores islas privadas del Pacífico Sur. Pohuenui ocupa 50 kilómetros de línea costera dibujada con bahías y playas

de arena, más de 45 kilómetros de caminos que conducen a granjas y caminos naturales que serpentean por un paisaje originario forrado de colinas y praderas. El punto más alto de la isla, a 600 metros, ofrece una panorámica espectacular a Marlborough Sound y las islas vecinas. El paisaje verde y montañoso con su gran diversidad de flora y fauna y un mar habitado por las más diversas especies de peces, delfines, focas y ballenas enamoran sin remedio a los amantes de la naturaleza. Con un poco de suerte, aquí se pueden incluso llegar a ver pingüinos, generalmente raros de encontrar. Lo que es seguro es que el visitante se topará al menos con una de las 3500 ovejas que habitan la isla.

Come un frammento delle Alpi precipitato nel Pacifico: è questa l'impressione che Pohuenui Island suscita dall'alto. Situata nel Marlborough Sound, la zona più soleggiata della Nuova Zelanda, Pohuenui, con oltre 2100 ettari di superficie, pari a dieci volte il principato di Monaco, è una delle isole private più grandi del Pacifico meridionale. Comprende 50 chilometri di costa con numerosi arenili, ed è percorsa da più di 45 chilometri di sentieri e strade naturali che si snodano nella natura selvaggia tra prati e colline. Dal punto più alto dell'isola, a 600 metri, si gode una fantastica vista sul Marlborough Sound e sulle vicine isole. Il paesaggio verde e selvaggio, la grande varietà della flora e della fauna, il mare ricco di pesci, i delfini, le foche e le balene incanteranno gli amanti della natura. Con un po' di fortuna si potrà anche incontrare un pinguino, animale raro su quest'isola, ma non mancherà occasione di fare la conoscenza di una delle 3500 pecore che vi vivono.

Fiji
Turtle Island

Movie-goers have already admired the snowy-white sand beaches and turquoise bays of Turtle Island on the big screen. The island, measuring 494 acres, with its twelve gorgeous beaches, hidden bays and palm trees swaying in the soft breeze was the location of the Hollywood movie "The Blue Lagoon".

Die schneeweißen Sandstrände und türkisfarbenen Buchten von Turtle Island waren schon auf der Kinoleinwand zu bewundern. Auf der 200 Hektar großen Insel mit ihren zwölf traumhaften Stränden, versteckten Buchten und sich in der sanften Brise wiegenden Palmen wurde der Hollywood-Film „Die Blaue Lagune" gedreht.

C'est sur les écrans de cinéma qu'il a été possible d'admirer les plages de sable blanc comme neige et les criques couleur turquoise de Turtle Island. Le film hollywoodien « Blue Lagoon » a effectivement été tourné sur les 200 hectares de cette grande île qui compte douze plages de rêve, des criques cachées et des palmiers qui se balancent au gré de la brise douce.

La blanca arena y las bahías color turquesa de Turtle Island se han disfrutado en la gran pantalla. En las 200 hectáreas con sus doce playas de ensueño y bahías escondidas en las que las palmeras se balancean al son de suaves brisas se filmó "El lago azul".

Le spiagge dalla sabbia bianchissima e le insenature turchine di Turtle Island hanno fatto da sfondo a diversi film. Su quest'isola di 200 ettari, con le sue dodici incantevoli spiagge, le baie nascoste e le palme che si curvano alla brezza leggera, è stato girato il film hollywoodiano "Laguna blu".

Turtle Island is part of the Yasawa group of the Fiji islands. The luxurious island resort is among the world's 300 best hotels. A maximum number of 28 guests—couples only— enjoy very personalized services. Turtle Island is the ideal setting for honeymooners who cherish romance.

Turtle Island gehört zur Yasawa-Gruppe der Fijis. Das luxuriöse Insel-Resort zählt zu den 300 besten Hotels der Welt, maximal 28 Gäste – ausschließlich Paare – genießen einen sehr persönlichen Service. Turtle Island ist ein idealer Ort für Honeymooner mit einem Sinn für Romantik.

Turtle Island fait partie du groupe Yasawa des Fidji. Le complexe hôtelier luxueux compte parmi les 300 meilleurs hôtels du monde. Là, un maximum de 28 hôtes – exclusivement des couples – bénéficient d'un service très personnalisé. Turtle Island est le lieu idéal pour ceux qui veulent passer une lune de miel avec une touche de romantisme.

Turtle Island pertenece al grupo Yasawa de las islas Fiji. El lujoso resort está considerado uno de los 300 mejores hoteles del mundo. No más de 28 huéspedes, siempre parejas, tienen la suerte de disfrutar de un servicio personalizado. Su sentido por el romanticismo hace de Turtle Island un lugar ideal para pasar la luna de miel.

Turtle Island fa parte del gruppo Yasawa delle isole Fiji. Il lussuoso resort dell'isola è uno dei 300 migliori hotel del mondo: gli ospiti, 28 persone al massimo, sono esclusivamente coppie, e godono di un servizio personalissimo. Turtle Island è il luogo ideale per un romantico viaggio di nozze.

French Polynesia, Tahiti
Motu Haapiti

A picture-book south-sea island. Its snowy-white sandy beaches, warm and shiny blue seas located in a magnificent lagoon, coupled with the luscious vegetation and a coral reef populated by exotic fish, all contribute to the particular charm of this small island.

Eine Südseeinsel wie aus dem Bilderbuch: Schneeweißer Sandstrand, warmes, leuchtend blaues Meerwasser in einer wunderschönen Lagune, eine üppige Vegetation und ein von exotischen Fischen bewohntes Korallenriff machen den Charme dieser kleinen Insel aus.

Cette île des mers du Sud semble sortir d'un livre d'images : une plage de sable blanc comme neige, une mer chaude et d'un bleu brillant dans une lagune merveilleuse, une végétation luxuriante et un récif corallien peuplé de poissons exotiques font le charme de cette petite île.

Una isla de ensueño. El encanto de este pequeño lugar se desprende de playas de arena blanca, aguas azules templadas y cristalinas, una fascinante laguna, vegetación exuberante y un arrecife de coral habitado por toda clase de especies exóticas.

Un'isola del sud come si vede solo nei libri illustrati: spiagge dalla sabbia bianca come la neve, una splendida laguna dall'acqua azzurrissima e calda, una vegetazione lussureggiante ed una barriera corallina in cui vivono specie di pesci esotici fanno di questa isoletta un luogo incantevole.

The bungalow, located on the island's northern side only a few steps away from the beach, presents impressive views of Bora Bora's volcanic cone and across the Pacific Ocean. Owner of this Tahitian island is the grandson of French polar explorer Paul-Émile Victor.

Beeindruckende Blicke auf den Vulkankegel von Bora Bora und über den Pazifischen Ozean hat man vom Bungalow auf der Inselnordseite – nur wenige Fuß-schritte vom Strand entfernt. Der Eigentümer dieser Tahiti-Insel ist der Enkel des französischen Polarforschers Paul-Émile Victor.

Le bungalow situé sur la face nord de l'île offre une vue impressionnante sur le cône volcanique de Bora Bora et sur l'océan Pacifique – à quelques pas de la plage. Le propriétaire de cette île de Tahiti est le petit-fils de l'explorateur polaire, Paul-Émile Victor.

A pocos pasos de la playa, desde el bungalow de la cara norte de la isla se aprecian las inigualables vistas al cono volcánico de Bora Bora y al Océano Pacífico. El propietario de esta isla de Tahití es el sobrino del investigador polar Paul-Émile Victor.

Dal bungalow situato nella parte settentrionale dell' isola, a pochi passi dalla spiaggia, si gode la vista mozzafiato del vulcano di Bora Bora e dell'oceano Pacifico. Il proprietario di questa isola dell'arcipelago di Tahiti è il nipote dell'esploratore polare francese Paul-Émile Victor.

French Polynesia, Bora Bora

Motu Tane

With a great deal of creativity, star make-up artist, photographer and cosmetics tycoon François Nars created on Motu Tane in the Bora Bora atoll his paradise on earth. He had hundreds of coconut palms planted and commissioned the construction of architecturally supreme elegant little villas and an outstandingly beautiful main house of precious wood whose side walls open or close in line with the weather situation.
In the year 1977, the famous French ethnologist and polar explorer Paul-Émile Victor settled on Motu Tane. During the quiet final part of his life he lived a simple lifestyle here and put his memories in writing. In the year 1995, at the age of 87, Victor died on his island.

Der Starvisagist, Fotograf und Kosmetikmogul François Nars schuf auf Motu Tane im Bora-Bora-Atoll mit viel Kreativität sein Paradies auf Erden. Er ließ Hunderte Kokospalmen pflanzen und errichtete auf architektonisch höchstem Niveau elegante kleine Villen und ein herausragend schönes Haupthaus aus Edelholz, dessen Seitenwände sich je nach Wetterlage öffnen oder schließen.
Im Jahr 1977 ließ sich der berühmte französische Ethnologe und Polarforscher Paul-Émile Victor auf Motu Tane nieder. Während seines ruhigen letzten Lebensabschnitts, ausgerichtet auf ein einfaches Dasein, brachte er hier seine Erinnerungen zu Papier. 1995 starb Victor auf seiner Insel im Alter von 87 Jahren.

Visagiste reconnu, photographe et roi de la cosmétique, François Nars a construit avec une grande créativité son paradis sur terre sur l'atoll de Bora Bora. Il a fait planter des centaines de cocotiers, bâtir d'élégantes petites villas du plus haut niveau architectonique et ériger une superbe résidence principale en bois précieux dont les parois latérales s'ouvrent et se ferment en fonction des conditions météorologiques.
En 1977, le célèbre ethnologue et explorateur polaire, Paul-Émile Victor, s'installa sur Motu Tane. Pendant la dernière partie calme de sa vie, orientée vers des besoins simples, il posa ses souvenirs sur le papier. Il est décédé sur son île en 1995 à l'âge de 87 ans.

El estilista de famosos, fotógrafo y magnate de la cosmética François Nars creó con ingenio su propio paraíso en Motu Tane, en el atolón de Bora Bora. Hizo plantar cientos de cocoteros y concibió elegantes y pequeñas villas al mayor nivel arquitectónico, además de un hermoso y amplio edificio principal de maderas nobles, cuyas paredes laterales se abren o cierran según las condiciones meteorológicas.

En el año 1977 el famoso etnólogo e investigador polar galo Paul-Émile Victor trasladó su residencia a Motu Tane. Durante los apacibles últimos años de su vida se centró en la esencia del vivir, y en este lugar plasmó en papel sus recuerdos. En 1995 Victor murió en la isla, a la edad de 87 años.

Il celebre visagista, fotografo e artista del make-up François Nars ha realizzato con grande creatività il proprio paradiso terrestre a Motu Tane, nell'atollo di Bora Bora. Vi ha fatto piantare centinaia di palme da cocco e costruire eleganti villette di squisita architettura, oltre ad una meravigliosa casa principale in legno pregiato, le cui pareti laterali si aprono e si chiudono secondo la situazione atmosferica.

Nel 1977, il famoso etnologo ed esploratore polare Paul-Émile Victor si è stabilito a Motu Tane. Durante gli ultimi, tranquilli anni della sua vita, trascorsi qui nella semplicità più assoluta, ha scritto le sue memorie. E nella sua isola Victor è morto nel 1995 all'età di 87 anni.

Life is very relaxed in the sand on Motu Tane—international guests from the photography, film and fashion scene have their breakfast on the beach under coconut palms, dine on an impressive precious wooden banquet table, and naturally let the evening fade away in the elegant lounge under the open sky.

Das Leben verläuft entspannt im Sand auf Motu Tane: Internationale Gäste aus der Fotografen-, Film- und Modeszene nehmen ihr Frühstück am Meeresstrand unter Kokospalmen ein, dinieren an einer imposanten Edelholztafel und lassen den Abend in der eleganten Lounge ausklingen – unter freiem Himmel, versteht sich.

La vie est relaxante sur le sable de Motu Tane : des hôtes internationaux de l'univers de la photographie, du film et de la mode prennent leur petit-déjeuner en bord de mer sous les cocotiers, dînent devant une table en bois précieux et laissent la soirée s'achever dans l'élégant salon à ciel ouvert, cela va de soi.

En la playa de Motu Tane la vida discurre relajadamente: huéspedes internacionales del mundo de la fotografía, del cine y de la moda desayunan a la orilla del mar bajo palmeras cocoteras, cenan en una impresionante mesa de madera noble y despiden la tarde en el elegante lounge, por supuesto a cielo abierto.

La vita trascorre in pieno relax sulla sabbia di Motu Tane: la clientela internazionale del mondo della fotografia, del cinema e della moda fa colazione sulla spiaggia all'ombra delle palme da cocco, si incontra a cena intorno a una ricca tavola di legno pregiato e conclude la serata nell'elegante cornice della lounge all'aperto.

Tiano Island

Tiano Island is an idyllic private island located in front of the western coast of Raiatea, "extended sky", the second-largest Society Island after Tahiti. Recent owners of the island included American soul singer Diana Ross and her husband Arne Naess as well as New Zealand businessman Douglas Myers.

Tiano Island ist eine idyllische Privatinsel vor der Westküste Raiateas, „Ausgedehnter Himmel", der nach Tahiti zweitgrößten der Gesellschaftsinseln. Die letzten Eigentümer der Insel waren die amerikanische Soul-Diva Diana Ross und ihr Ehemann Arne Naess sowie der neuseeländische Geschäftsmann Douglas Myers.

Tiano Island est une île privée idyllique située devant la côte occidentale de Raiatea, « vaste ciel », la plus grande des îles de la Société après Tahiti. La diva américaine de la soul musique, Diana Ross, et sont époux, Arne Naess, ainsi que Douglas Myers, homme d'affaires néo-zélandais étaient les derniers propriétaires de l'île.

Tiano Island es una idílica isla privada, ubicada en la costa oeste de Raiatea, "el cielo alargado", y, tras Tahití, la segunda más grande de las islas de la sociedad. Los últimos propietarios de la isla fueron la diva del soul Diana Ross y su esposo Arne Naess, así como el empresario neozelandés Douglas Myers.

Tiano Island è un'idilliaca isola privata situata di fronte alla costa occidentale di Raiatea, "cielo immenso", la più grande delle Isole della Società dopo Tahiti. Gli ultimi proprietari dell'isola sono stati la diva del soul americana Diana Ross, suo marito Arne Naess e l'uomo di affari neozelandese Douglas Myers.

The luxurious, yet understated residential building was constructed exclusively from the island's indigenous materials and is situated inside a tropical garden.

Das luxuriöse, doch dezente Wohnhaus ist ausschließlich aus inseleigenem Material erbaut worden und liegt in einem tropischen Garten.

L'habitation luxueuse, mais décente a été construite avec des matériaux exclusivement trouvés sur l'île et se situe dans un jardin tropical.

La lujosa y a la vez discreta vivienda está construida básicamente con materiales de la isla e insertada en un jardín tropical.

La lussuosa e sobria abitazione è stata costruita esclusivamente con materiale originario dell'isola nel mezzo di un giardino tropicale.

French Polynesia, Tahiti
Tetiaroa Atoll

Marlon Brando discovered the beauty of Polynesia in the early 1960's during the shooting of the film classic "Mutiny on the Bounty". Brando found his personal paradise on the Society Island Tetiaroa Atoll, "The Bird Island", located 26 miles north of Tahiti. He purchased the island from a British dentist. Until his death in the year 2004, Brando held a protective hand over the island and financed environmental protection projects on the coral archipelago. Tetiaroa Atoll was once the hideaway of the Tahitian royal family. This was the site where they fattened their women until they matched the full-bodied beauty ideal of their time.

Marlon Brando entdeckte die Schönheit Polynesiens Anfang der sechziger Jahre während der Dreharbeiten zu dem Filmklassiker „Meuterei auf der Bounty". Auf der Gesellschaftsinsel Tetiaroa, „Die Vogelinsel", 42 Kilometer nördlich von Tahiti gelegen, fand Brando sein persönliches Paradies; er erwarb die Insel von einem englischen Zahnarzt. Bis Brando im Jahre 2004 verstarb, hielt er seine schützende Hand über die Insel und finanzierte auf dem Korallenarchipel Umweltschutzprojekte. Tetiaroa war einst Refugium der tahitianischen Königsfamilie: Hier mästeten sie ihre Frauen, damit sie dem wohlgenährten Schönheitsideal entsprachen.

Marlon Brando découvrit la beauté de la Polynésie au début des années 1960 pendant le tournage du grand classique « Les Révoltés du Bounty ». Brando trouva son paradis personnel sur l'île de la Société Tetiaroa Atoll, « l'île aux oiseaux », située à 42 kilomètres au nord de Tahiti ; il l'acheta à un dentiste anglais. Jusqu'à sa mort en 2004, Brando protégea l'île et finança des projets de protection de l'environnement sur l'archipel corallien. Tetiaroa Atoll était autrefois le refuge de la famille royale tahitienne : là, ils engraissaient leurs femmes afin qu'elles correspondent à leur idéal de beauté.

Marlon Brando descubrió la belleza de Polinesia a comienzos de los años sesenta, durante el rodaje del clásico del celuloide, "El motín de la Bounty". En la isla de la sociedad Tetiaroa Atoll, "la isla de los pájaros", 42 kilómetros al norte de Tahití, Brando encontró su paraíso personal. El lugar se lo compró a un dentista británico. Hasta su muerte en el año 2004, Brando ejerció de mano protectora y financió diversos proyectos para la conservación del medio ambiente en el archipiélago de coral. Tetiaroa Atoll en su día fue refugio de la familia real tahitiana. Aquí los hombres cebaban a sus mujeres para que estuvieran bien alimentadas y correspondieran así al ideal de belleza.

Marlon Brando ha scoperto la bellezza della Polinesia all'inizio degli anni sessanta, durante le riprese del celebre film "Gli ammutinati del Bounty". A Tetiaroa Atoll, "l'isola degli uccelli", una delle Isole della Società, a 42 chilometri a nord di Tahiti, Brando trovò il proprio paradiso personale: acquistò l'isola da un dentista inglese. Fino alla sua morte, avvenuta nel 2004, Brando ha protetto l'isola finanziando progetti di salvaguardia dell'ambiente nell'arcipelago corallino. Tetiaroa Atoll è stata un tempo il rifugio della famiglia reale di Tahiti: qui le donne venivano fatte ingrassare affinché corrispondessero all'ideale di bellezza prosperosa comune in questi luoghi.

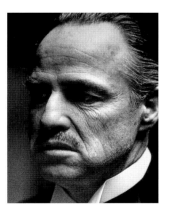

INDEX

Choice of rental islands in this book:

Bahamas

Musha Cay, Great Exuma
Musha Cay—the most luxurious island resort in the world. 5 elegant villas for up to 25 guests, each with own private beach.
Guide Price: from USD 24,750 to USD 44,500 per night, all-inclusive

Little Whale Cay, Berry Islands
A Garden of Eden only 20 flight minutes from Nassau, island's own airstrip, private harbor with island chapel (weddings). 3 generous guest houses for up to 12 people, chef and staff fulfill each wish. Ideal base for all watersports—equipment available.
Guide Price: from USD 55,000 per week for the entire island

Bonefish Cay, Abacos
The Bahamas—exclusive and private for up to 16 guests. 3 villas, large main house, extravagant and modern technical facilities. Gourmet excursion according to your request.
Guide Price: EUR 45,000 per week including full board, service, use of boats and existing equipment

British Virgin Islands

Necker Island
Exclusivity for up to 26 guests. 10-bedroom main house with living room, jacuzzi, and private terrace. Authentic Balinese homes Bali Hi, Bali Cliff and Bali Lo offer elegant villa accommodation with private pools, open-air lounges, and private dining areas. Services from A to Z.
Guide Price: from USD 42,500 per day for the entire island

Guana Island
Tropical island paradise for a maximum of 30 guests, just a few minutes by boat from Tortola, 865 acres of pure nature with pretty coves surrounded by turquoise waters.
Guide Price: from USD 650 to USD 900 per day per cottage including full board as well as all island activities, from USD 1,200 per day for the exclusive North Beach Cottage, from USD 13,500 per day for the entire island

Curaçao

Spanish Water Cay
Undisturbed holiday and privacy guaranteed. Generous villa complex amidst colorful palm gardens, motorboat for day trips available, swimming, snorkelling, diving, sailing.
Guide Price: rental on request

Chile

Isla Robinson Crusoe
The island is accessed via Santiago (about 3-hour flight in a small charter plane). 2 guest houses offer clean and simple rooms and a comfortable atmosphere.
Guide Price: from USD 140 per day per person

Canada

Sleepy Cove Island, Nova Scotia
Romantic Canadian log home with wonderful sun terrace offering spectacular views of the lake, self-catering, canoe tours, swimming, fishing and much more.
Guide Price: from CAD 165 per day for the entire island

USA

East Brother Island, California
A lighthouse island with flair in the middle of the San Francisco Bay. Exclusive Victorian-style hostel with ocean views, next to the lively metropole of San Francisco.
Guide Price: from USD 350 per night for 2 people

Dark Island, Upstate New York

Be King or Queen of your own castle on a private island in the picturesque Thousand Islands region in the Saint Lawrence River. You will reside in the only exclusive suite with breathtaking views. Weddings, family celebrations or business events in the great hall, castle terrace or in the tea garden.
Guide Price: from USD 650 per night for the VIP suite, exclusive booking of the castle and island possible

Melody Key, Florida

Your own private island kingdom in the Florida Keys, only 15 miles from Key West. Exclusive island villa for up to 6 guests.
Guide Price: from USD 7,800 to USD 9,500 per week

Spain

Tago Mago, Ibiza

Located approximately one mile east of the shore of Ibiza with large traditional villa. Comfortable accommodation for up to 8 guests. Services provided by staff. Rental on request.

Isla de sa Ferradura, Ibiza

The most exclusive rental island in Europe. Over 30 members of staff care for up to 14 guests. Magnificent and luxurious villa complex with 7 suites, spa, pools, fitness center, gardens. A private marina and transport fleet available for day trips. Ideal location and unique surroundings for festivities, weddings and company events.
Guide Price: 6 guests low season May and Oct.
EUR 64,000/week (all-inclusive) plus VAT 16%,
14 guests same period EUR 109,000/week (all-inclusive) plus VAT 16%
6 guests peak season July – Aug. EUR 73,000/week (all-inclusive) plus VAT 16%, 14 guests same peak period EUR 126,000/week (all-inclusive) plus VAT 16%
Special rebates possible for early bookings.

France

Île de Chantemesle

10-acre paradise in one of the most magical regions near Paris between La Roche Guyon and Vétheuil. Generous villa for 12 guests. Only 45 minutes from the city center of Paris—a beautiful alternative to a city hotel.
Guide Price: depending on season, EUR 5,000 to EUR 8,000 per week

Great Britain

Tresco Island, Isles of Scilly

Rent one of the cosy traditional-style cottages. Or stay in the popular island hotel directly on the beach with breathtaking views of the Atlantic.
Guide Price: double room in the island hotel from GBP 150 to GBP 240 (incl. breakfast and dinner). Cottages from GBP 800 to GBP 2,200 per week

Ireland

Horse Island

An Irish nature paradise away from mass tourism. 3 large and tastefully decorated stone cottages for a maximum of 12 guests. Private sauna with ocean views, whirlpool. Ideal destination for honeymooners, nature lovers and those seeking a little peace and quiet.
Guide Price: EUR 2,000 per cottage per week

Waterford Castle

A golf paradise with Victorian glamour. Castle hotel with 19 rooms and marvelous views for relaxing holidays as well as for conferences and festivities. Golf in Waterford Golf & Country Club (18-hole course), clay-pigeon shooting, pheasant and duck hunting, horse-riding, polo, heated swimming pool, bowling.
Guide Price: from EUR 200 to EUR 600 per room per night

Seychelles

Frégate Island

16 luxurious separate villas hidden between palm trees on the island coastline with fantastic views of the sea: 2800 square feet fitted out in mahogany, bamboo, marble, and equipped with fine modern technical facilities. International top chef as well as an exquisite wine menu guarantee a gourmet delight.
Guide Price: USD 1,800 to USD 2,100 per day per villa including full board

Cousine Island

Unique and precious nature reserve and guaranteed privacy. 4 villas in French colonial style, main house with bar, lounge, library and large swimming pool. Dine on the beach and enjoy a romantic dinner under the stars.

Guide Price: EUR 1,400 per villa per night, rental of the entire island from EUR 5,000 per night

North Island

Oasis of peace with understated luxury. 10 Presidential Villas designed in a mixture of traditional Bali and Seychelles-style, each with own pool. Exclusive highlight is villa No. 11, Villa North. French-Creole and international cuisine. Wellness spa on the granite rocks with fantastic views.

Guide Price: EUR 1,250 per person/per night all inclusive. EUR 3,500 – 4,000 per night for 4 people in a Royal or North Island Villa

Chauve Souris Island

Small dream island especially for honeymooners. Only 5 specially designed rooms: Pirate Room, Admirals Room, Ladies Room, Shipwrecked-Bungalow and Countryman Room. The Pirate Room was built into a rock formation on the island, the Shipwrecked-Bungalow is positioned in a lonely location.

Guide Price: from EUR 360 per day per person including full board and open island bar

Maldives

Soneva Fushi

Kunfunadhoo at 4,600 feet long and almost 1,312 feet wide is one of the largest islands in the Maldives. Various styles of villas on the beach and on stilts. Open concept with patios, jacuzzis, private gardens and beaches. Excellent and internationally well-known Six Senses Spa. Ultimate hideaways are the Soneva Fushi Retreat and The Jungle Reserve with private massage pavilion, main house, master bedroom villa, pool and the special Tree House.

Guide Price: from USD 500 to USD 2,000 per night per villa, Soneva Retreat USD 3,500 per night, Jungle Reserve USD 5,000 per night

Soneva Gili

The first totally-overwater-bungalow-resort in the Maldives, set on the private tropical island of Lankanfushi. The 29 Soneva Gili Villa Suites and 8 Soneva Gili Residences are located in such a way that total privacy is guaranteed. 7 Crusoe Residences are situated in the lagoon looking out to the coral reef and open ocean. An exclusive highlight is the Private Reserve—a fantastic villa complex built on stilts, 1,640 feet away from the island.

Guide Price: from USD 645 to USD 1,540 per night per villa, Private Reserve from USD 10,000 per day for up to 8 guests

Australia

Bedarra Island, Great Barrier Reef

About 90 miles north of Townsville on the Great Barrier Reef. 16 spacious villas designed to blend in with the beauty of their natural surrounding, with own balcony or terrace. 3 brand new luxury villas separate from one another, designed using elements of glass and wood.

Guide Price: per day and per person including full board and diverse sport activities, from AUD 950 per Bay Villa per night, from AUD 1,450 per Hideaway Villa per night

New Zealand

Forsyth Island, Marlborough Sound

An entire private island kingdom of 2,100 acres for a dream holiday. Exclusive lodge with 2,580 square feet living space, 3 bedrooms with ensuite bathrooms, modern kitchen, dining room, generous living area with cathedral ceiling, terrace surrounding the house and offering marvellous panoramic views. Boat tours, fishing trips, whale and dolphin watching, swimming, kayaking and surfing. The island's impressive cuisine attracts much praise with traditional menus, fresh fish and seafood and the produce of the island's garden, served with the finest New Zealand wines.

Guide Price: from EUR 1000 to EUR 1,500 per day for the rental of the entire island for between 6 to 8 guests

Pohuenui Island, Marlborough Sound

With approximately 5,190 acres, Pohuenui is one of the largest privately-owned islands in the South Pacific. The traditional farmhouse with 4 bedrooms nestles in the middle of a botanical garden. The exclusive and captivating guesthouse with 3 bedrooms is located in a pretty cove in Garden Bay on the other side of the island.

Bookings on self-catering or full board basis.

Guide Price: Rental of each house from EUR 500 to EUR 1,000 for 6 to 8 guests per day

Fiji

Turtle Island

A wonderful haven for a maximum of 28 guests. Enjoy the very personal service of the friendly hosts, who are available around the clock and eager to fulfill every wish. Perfect location for weddings and honeymooners. 14 Polynesian-style, beachfront bures, with queen or king-size four-poster beds, sitting-room, two bathrooms, well-stocked refridgerators and other amenities.

Guide Price: depending on season and number of travelers: from USD 1,600/Deluxe Bure per day (including full board, all services, use of all equipment and excursions). Grand Bure from USD 1,900. Vonu Point from USD 2,300. All rates plus local taxes.

French Polynesia

Motu Tane, Bora Bora

An exceptionally beautiful island just minutes away from the main island of Bora Bora. Private hideaway for exclusive parties for up to 26 guests. 2 expansive master suites (2,500 sqare feet.), 2 separate suites on the sunrise and the sunset sides of the island and 9 suites along the pretty sand beaches. Interiors designed by world class designer Christian Liaigre. Excellent chef service and marvelous watersports.

Guide Price: from USD 200,000 per week

Booking contact:

VLADI PRIVATE ISLANDS
Ballindamm 7
20095 Hamburg
Germany
Tel: +49 40 33 00 00
Fax: +49 40 33 00 81
e-mail: travel@vladi.de

VLADI PRIVATE ISLANDS
Historic Properties Suite 158
1869 Upper Water Street
Halifax Nova Scotia B3J 1S9
Canada
Tel: +1 902 423 3202
Fax: +1 902 425 4765
e-mail: travel@vladi.de

IMPRINT

Editor: Farhad Vladi
Wolfgang Behnken,
www.funk-behnken.de

Art Director: Wolfgang Behnken/Funk+Behnken

Layout: Constanze Lemke/Funk+Behnken
Aline Hoffbauer, Ingrid Nündel/
querformat design

Illustrations: Nicole Krohn

Text: Martina Matthiesen, Firouz Vladi,
Farhad Vladi

Translations: SAW Communications,
Dr. Sabine A. Werner, Mainz
Cosima Talhouni (English)
Sabine Boccador (French)
Maider Olarra (Spanish)
Maria-Letizia Haas (Italian)

Edited by: Nina Tebartz/teNeues Verlag
Andreas Feßer

Second Edition

© 2007 teNeues Verlag GmbH + Co. KG, Kempen

Production by Dieter Haberzettl, teNeues Verlag
Pre-press by Medien Team-Vreden, Germany

Photo credits:

Bedarra Island, p 14, 16, 184-185
Camera Press London, p 127
Chauve Souris Island, p 12, 142, 168
Corbis, p 35, 39, 61, 78, 100, 111, 119, 211, 215
Cousine Island, p 162-163
Einzig, Dan, p 30-31
Frégate Island Private, back cover bottom, p 156-159
Guana Island, p 46-49
Horse Island, p 133, 134
Île de Chantemesle, p 112-113
Isla de sa Ferradura, p 97
Kiattipong Panchhee for Soneva Fushi/Gili, p 8, 18,
    174-177, 180-181
Kullberg, Dan, cover, p 170, 179, © Six Senses Hotels
    Resorts & Spas
Lassa/Robinson Crusoe Tours, p 56-59
Matthiesen, Martina, p 6, 135
Melody Key, p 86-87
Motu Tane, p 146, 207-209
Musha Cay, p 10, 24-27
Nova Scotia Tourism Board, p 85
Picture-Alliance/Photoshot, p 83
Proust, Alain, p 38-45
Schonart, Ulli, p 171-172, 173 bottom, 178, © Six Senses
    Hotels Resorts & Spas
Spanish Water Cay, p 50-53
Taprobane Island, p 144
Tiano Island, p 212-213, by kind permission of Arne Ness.
Tresco Island, p 128-131
Turtle Island, p 196-199
Waterford Castle, p 136-139
Zack, Memo, p 173 top, © Six Senses Hotels
    Resorts & Spas
All rights reserved.

All other photos by Farhad Vladi.
© 2006 Dr. Farhad Vladi.
All rights reserved.

Published by teNeues Publishing Group

teNeues Verlag GmbH + Co. KG
Am Selder 37, 47906 Kempen, Germany
Tel.: 0049 / 2152 / 916 - 0
Fax: 0049 / 2152 / 916 - 111
e-mail: books@teneues.de
Press department: arehn@teneues.de
Tel.: 0049 / 2152 / 916 - 202

teNeues Publishing Company
16 West 22nd Street, New York, N.Y. 10010, USA
Tel.: 001 / 212 / 627 9090
Fax: 001 / 212 / 627 9511

teNeues Publishing UK Ltd.
P.O. Box 402, West Byfleet, KT14 7ZF, Great Britain
Tel.: 0044 / 1932 / 403509
Fax: 0044 / 1932 / 403514

teNeues France S.A.R.L.
93, rue Bannier, 45000 Orléans, France
Tel.: 0033 / 2 / 38541071
Fax: 0033 / 2 / 38625340

www.teneues.com

Bibliographic information published by Die Deutsche
Bibliothek.
Die Deutsche Bibliothek lists this publication in the
Deutsche Nationalbibliografie; detailed bibliographic data is
available in the Internet at http://dnb.ddb.de.

ISBN: 978-3-8327-9110-0

Printed in Italy